As one of the world's longest established and best-known travel brands, Thomas Cook are the experts in travel.

For more than 135 years our guidebooks have unlocked the secrets of destinations around the world, sharing with travellers a wealth of experience and a passion for travel.

Rely on Thomas Cook as your travelling companion on your next trip and benefit from our unique heritage.

D0877158

Thomas Cook **traveller** guides

JORDAN
Diana Darke

HALF HOLLOW HILLS
COMMUNITY LIBRARY
55 Vanderbilt Parkway
Dix Hills, NY 11746

Your travelling companion since 1873

Thomas Cook

Written and updated by Diana Darke
Original photography by Diana Darke

Published by Thomas Cook Publishing
A division of Thomas Cook Tour Operations Limited
Company registration no. 3772199 England
The Thomas Cook Business Park, Unit 9, Coningsby Road,
Peterborough PE3 8SB, United Kingdom
Email: books@thomascook.com, Tel: +44 (0) 1733 416477
www.thomascookpublishing.com

Produced by Cambridge Publishing Management Limited
Burr Elm Court, Main Street, Caldecote CB23 7NU
www.cambridgepm.co.uk

ISBN: 978-1-84848-447-4

© 2007, 2009 Thomas Cook Publishing
This third edition © 2011
Text © Thomas Cook Publishing
Maps © Thomas Cook Publishing/PCGraphics (UK) Limited

Series Editor: Karen Beaulah
Production/DTP: Steven Collins

Printed and bound in Spain by GraphyCems

Cover photography © Eric Nathan/Alamy

All rights reserved. No part of this publication may be reproduced, stored in a retrieval system or transmitted, in any form or by any means, electronic, mechanical, recording or otherwise, in any part of the world, without prior permission of the publisher. Requests for permission should be made to the publisher at the above address.

Although every care has been taken in compiling this publication, and the contents are believed to be correct at the time of printing, Thomas Cook Tour Operations Limited cannot accept any responsibility for errors or omissions, however caused, or for changes in details given in the guidebook, or for the consequences of any reliance on the information provided. Descriptions and assessments are based on the author's views and experiences when writing and do not necessarily represent those of Thomas Cook Tour Operations Limited.

Contents

Introduction

Jordan contains, within its small and random boundaries, a remarkable collection of dramatic contrasts, packaged in digestible form for the visitor. Everyone knows of Petra, the 'rose-red city half as old as time', and maybe even Wadi Rum, famed for its Lawrence of Arabia associations. But ask anyone to name another site and they almost invariably fumble, unable to bring to mind the Roman cities, Crusader castles, Christian settlements and mosaics, let alone the quixotic Arab desert palaces that Jordan also boasts.

Many are surprised to learn that Jordan consists in large part of a high plateau some 700–1,000m (2,300–3,280ft) above sea level, where its capital Amman sits, making it the second highest capital in the Middle East, after Sana'a in Yemen. From Amman you can drive in under an hour down to the Dead Sea at about 400m (1,300ft) below sea level. Jordanian landscapes range from the forested highlands of the north to the subtropical Jordan Valley, and from the eerie eroded mountains of Petra and Wadi Rum to the flat basalt deserts in the east towards the Iraqi and Saudi borders. The population encompasses some of the few remaining desert-dwelling Bedouin left in the Arab world, along with some of the region's most highly educated and sophisticated workforce, resident largely in Amman.

The variety on offer in terms of sightseeing is greater even than that of Egypt. Visitors can, in the space of a few days, walk along the intact streets of Roman Jerash, discover the intriguing Arab palaces of the desert, visit wildlife reserves and marvel at superbly preserved Christian mosaics and dramatically perched hilltop Crusader castles. They can then go on horseback through the narrow defile of Petra to be confronted with the Treasury, one of the most spectacular sites in the world, ride a camel through the haunting moonscapes of Wadi Rum, and round off the experience with the sandy beaches and colourful marine life of the Red Sea coral reefs at Aqaba.

Jordan's identity has been defined on the world stage more than anything by its royal family, the Hashemites, a dynasty originating in the Hejaz, Saudi Arabia, and tracing itself back to the Prophet Muhammad. King Hussein, who ruled Jordan for 46 years until his death in 1999, was the 42nd-generation direct descendant of the Prophet. His son Abdullah is the current king, born of an English mother, King Hussein's second wife. His is the tricky job of maintaining the country's peace agreement with Israel and its close ties with the US, unpopular with many Jordanians.

With no oil of its own, the country is heavily dependent on aid, mainly from the US, but is looking increasingly to tourism to help boost its economy. Of paramount importance therefore is the country's image to the West as a safe and stable tourist destination, which it takes great care to foster, despite the occasional setback from terrorist incidents. Projected as a friend of the West, unlike its less fortunate neighbour Syria, Jordan is hoping that Petra's success in the Seven New Wonders of the World competition (along with the Taj Mahal and Macchu Picchu) will continue to secure much-needed tourism investment for the future.

Introduction

Amman's huge Raghadan flagpole can be seen from all over the city

The land

Jordan is a small country, roughly the size of Ireland, a tenth the size of Egypt, and a fifth the size of France. Yet within its constraining borders, arrived at through the whims of foreign, mainly British, policies after World War I, Jordan offers surprising contrasts in landscape and hence in climate. Lack of water is a major problem for Jordan's plans to increase agricultural development, and, as a result, the country is far from self-sufficient in food, especially wheat.

Regions

Jordan's only natural topographical border is its western one, represented initially by the River Jordan. It rises just inside Syria from the snows of Mount Hermon, before flowing through Israel's Lake Tiberias (Sea of Galilee), then through the Jordan Valley where it disgorges into the Dead Sea, 251km (156 miles) later. The border then runs straight through the middle of the Dead Sea, giving both Jordan and Israel their respective shorelines, before continuing southwards in the form of the Wadi Araba, which ends at the Red Sea and the port of Aqaba.

The north–south Wadi Araba is in fact a continuation of the East African Rift Valley, the longest and deepest scar in the earth's surface, running from Africa 6,440km (4,000 miles) up through Syria, ending in the mountainous province of Hatay in southern Turkey. The fault line means that the region still has minor earthquakes from time to time, and the great quantities of lava that swelled up have covered large expanses of Syria and Jordan with black basalt desert. A shift in the Jordan Valley fault line was

---

COUNTRY FACTS

Area 89,213sq km (34,445sq miles)
Coastline 26km (16 miles)
Highest point Jebel Rum 1,754m (5,755ft)
Lowest point Dead Sea –408m (–1,339ft)

Population Approximately 6.5 million, of whom some 40 per cent are refugees (UN). The population is 98 per cent Arab, 1 per cent Circassian, 1 per cent Armenian. Of the Arabs: 2 million Palestinian, half a million Iraqi, the rest Jordanian
Life expectancy 72 years for men, 76 years for women (UN)
Religion 92 per cent Sunni Muslim, 6 per cent Christian, 2 per cent other

Natural resources Phosphates, potash, shale oil
Main exports Phosphate, fertilisers, agricultural products
Land use Permanent pastures 9 per cent, arable land 4 per cent, permanent crops 1 per cent, forests and woodland 1 per cent, other 85 per cent

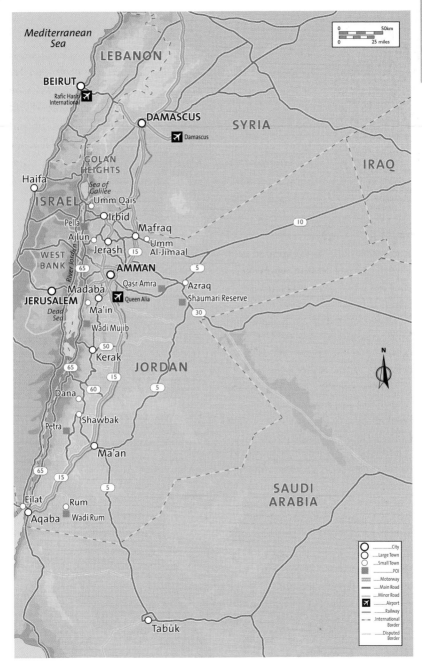

Mediterranean Sea

LEBANON

BEIRUT
Rafic Hariri International

DAMASCUS

SYRIA

Damascus

IRAQ

GOLAN HEIGHTS

Haifa

Sea of Galilee

Umm Qais

ISRAEL

Pella

Irbid

Mafraq

Ajlun

Jerash

15

Umm Al-Jimaal

WEST BANK

65

River Jordan

AMMAN

5

Madaba

Qasr Amra

Azraq

JERUSALEM

Queen Alia

Shaumari Reserve

Dead Sea

Ma'in

30

Wadi Mujib

50

65

Kerak

JORDAN

15

60

5

Dana

Shawbak

Petra

Ma'an

65

15

5

N

Eilat

Rum

Aqaba

Wadi Rum

SAUDI ARABIA

◎	...............City
◉	....Large Town
○	....Small Town
■	...............POI
	....Motorway
	....Main Road
	...Minor Road
✈	...........Airport
	...........Railway
	.International Border
	.....Disputed Border

Tabūk

0 50km
0 25 miles

10

thought to have been the cause of the 1927 earthquakes which led to extensive damage in Amman.

Apart from this great valley and the small amount of coastline around the port of Aqaba on the Red Sea, the remaining 85 per cent of Jordan consists of a huge, high plateau ranging between 700 and 1,000m (2,300 and 3,280ft) in altitude. The plateau continues into Syria to the north, and into Iraq and Saudi Arabia to the east. The plateau is not entirely flat; it has many dramatic hilly sections, notably in Amman, which is built on a series of hills, and at Wadi Rum, where the impressive mountains culminate in Jordan's highest peak, Jebel Rum, at 1,754m (5,755ft). Jordan also has a number of mineral springs and areas of forest, especially in the northern hills.

Climate

The contrast in landscape is reflected climatically within the kingdom, with the towering plateau leading to cool breezes and cooler nights even in the height of summer. The Jordan Valley and Aqaba have a semi-tropical climate, while the desert proper has the typical extremes of very hot days and very cold nights. Spring and autumn are the best times to visit, specifically March, April, October and early November, when daytime temperatures are pleasantly low at around 20°C (68°F), which is excellent for sightseeing.

Water and agriculture

As it is in limited supply, Jordan's water has to be carefully managed to ensure it is constantly available for drinking

The valleys and mountains of northwestern Jordan

The Wadi As-Sir is one of Jordan's more fertile areas

and that wastewater is recycled for agricultural use. The country is served by two main rivers, the Jordan and the Yarmouk, but both are heavily exploited upstream by Israel and Syria respectively. Jordan's King Abdullah and Syria's President Bashar Al-Assad have, however, shared the cost of Al-Wahda Dam (Unity Dam), built on their shared border, from which Jordan takes the water and Syria the hydroelectric power. Further south, close to the Saudi border, the Disi aquifer is also being tapped but is a non-replenishable source; at the expected rate of usage its supplies will last 50 years. Jordan remains hopeful that the Red Sea-Dead Sea Canal project (*see p75*), complete with its own desalination plants, will one day be implemented and that it will be able to provide for all of the country's future water needs.

Changed boundaries

Jordan lost the West Bank and East Jerusalem in the disastrous 1967 war with Israel and they remain today under Israeli military occupation, awaiting a peace settlement with the Palestinians. Israel refers to the West Bank in biblical terms as Judea and Samaria. Syria's Golan Heights and Egypt's Sinai Peninsula and Gaza Strip were both lost in the same war, but while Egypt regained Sinai in the Camp David peace deal, the Golan is unlikely to be surrendered since it provides two thirds of Israel's water supplies.

History

50,000–4000 BC First sedentary villages and beginnings of agriculture in Jordan, as evidenced by hunting tools found in Wadi Rum and Azraq.

1250–1200 BC According to the Old Testament, Moses and the Israelites' exodus from Egypt. Joshua captures Jericho and divides Palestine among the 12 tribes of Israel.

1200–539 BC Kingdoms of Ammon, Moab and Edom, east of the Jordan and the Wadi Araba, in constant conflict with the Israelites. 800–539 BC: Assyrian and Babylonian conquests in Jordan.

538 BC Nabateans come to power in the south of Jordan, with their capital at Petra.

332 BC Alexander the Great takes Palestine.

63 BC Romans led by Pompey conquer Palestine and Jerusalem.

63 BC–AD 106 The Decapolis, a federation of ten cities now in Jordan, is attached to the Roman Province of Syria and lasts until around AD 106.

37 BC–AD 4 Herod the Great, of Edomite origins but converted to Judaism, is king of the Jews.

AD 106 Rome conquers Nabatean kingdom and joins it to the Province of Arabia.

324 Christianity is established as the state religion of the Roman Empire.

636 Battle of Yarmouk: Byzantines defeated by Arabs and forced to evacuate Jordan, Palestine and Syria. Jordan submits to Islam.

661–750 Umayyad dynasty of Muslim caliphs rules with Damascus as its capital.

1095–1187 The Crusades. 1099: Jerusalem captured by the Crusaders. 1171–87: Saladin recaptures Jerusalem and his Ayyubid dynasty rules the region.

1263–1516 Mamelukes, under Baybars of Egypt, rule the region.

1520–66	Suleyman the Magnificent extends the Ottoman Empire over all Arabia.
1916	Ottoman Empire sides with Germany in World War I, and faces the Arab Revolt of the tribes seeking their independence.
1917–18	Arabs take Aqaba. Allies take Jerusalem. Ottoman domination ends.
1920–46	Transjordan and Palestine placed under British mandate.
1947	Hashemite Kingdom of Jordan created.
1948	State of Israel created in British-mandate Palestine. First wave of Palestinian refugees flee to the West Bank and Jordan.
1950	Jordan annexes the West Bank and East Jerusalem.
1951	King Abdullah I assassinated in Jerusalem during prayers at the Al-Aqsa mosque.
1952	Hussein becomes king aged 17, after his father Talal's one-year rule and abdication.
1967	Six Day War. Israel seizes the West Bank and Jerusalem from Jordan, along with the Gaza Strip and Sinai from Egypt and the Golan Heights from Syria.
1980–88	Iran–Iraq War. Jordan sides with Iraq, which uses Aqaba port for supplies.
1990–91	Iraq invades Kuwait, leading to US attack. Jordan isolated from rest of Arab world after refusing to condemn Saddam Hussein.
1994	Jordan signs peace treaty with Israel, ending the 46-year official state of war. Jordan regains US aid.
1999	King Hussein dies. His son Abdullah becomes king, not Crown Prince Hassan.
2000–2009	Isolated terrorist incidents damage Jordan's image as a safe tourist destination.
2007	Petra is named one of the New Seven Wonders of the World by UNESCO.
2011	King Abdullah II sacks his cabinet and brings in new constitutional reforms in response to demonstrations.

T E Lawrence and the Arab Revolt

Disillusioned by years of backward Ottoman rule, by 1914 the Arabs had reached the stage where they were prepared to take united action. Under the Hashemite Sherif Hussein of the Hejaz, the previously disparate tribes joined together to fulfil a dream of Arab unity and independence and to rid themselves of the Ottomans.

Encouraged by the Allies, who were already fighting the Ottoman enemy in the war, and in particular by T E Lawrence, Hussein was given to understand that Britain would back him if the Arabs he commanded fought with the Allies against their Ottoman oppressors. The extent of the new Arab empire was to

Qasr Azraq, where T E Lawrence was based

LAWRENCE'S STING

Sherif Ali: 'There is the railway. And that is the desert. From here until we reach the other side, no water but what we carry with us. For the camels, no water at all. If the camels die, we die. And in 20 days they will start to die.'

Lawrence: 'There's no time to waste, then, is there?'

As Auda Abu Tayi, sheikh of the Howaytat tribe, said to Lawrence: 'Thy mother mated with a scorpion.'

encompass all countries between Egypt and Persia, with the exception of imperial possessions and interests in Kuwait, Aden and the Syrian coast.

Captain T E Lawrence was the young British officer sent from Egypt to work with the Arabs and to convince them to unite and coordinate their actions in support of British strategy. Their constant raids against Ottoman positions weakened the opposition and provided the Allies under General Allenby with intelligence on Ottoman army positions, which then enabled them to take Jerusalem in 1917 and Damascus in 1918. By the end of the war they had driven back the Ottomans and seized what today constitutes Palestine, Jordan, Lebanon, large parts of the Arabian Peninsula and southern Syria.

Despite the Arabs' great success, it transpired that Britain and France had met secretly a month earlier and already agreed to divide between themselves the lands they had earlier promised to Sherif Hussein and his sons Faisal and Abdullah. After the war, Iraq, Palestine and Jordan were duly put under British mandate, while Syria and Lebanon were allocated to the French. The majority of Arabs felt betrayed. Even Churchill referred to Britain's conduct as 'a confusion of principles' and Lawrence called it 'a despicable fraud'. The British had broken their wartime promises, a betrayal which was compounded by the 1917 Balfour Declaration supporting the establishment of a national home for the Jews in Palestine. It was in partial recognition of this earlier betrayal that Churchill, as Colonial Secretary in 1921, agreed to allow the separate mandate of Transjordan (*see pp14*) to be established under the administration of Abdullah, Sherif Hussein's son.

DEATH KNELL TO ARAB UNITY

In his autobiography *Uneasy Lies the Head* (1962), King Hussein describes the failure of the Arab Revolt as the death knell of Arab unity. Since then, he says, the various Arab countries have pulled apart, finding it impossible to forget their domestic ambitions. 'As people we are one, seeking the same goal. As nations we lose each other down the different paths by which we choose to fulfil our national objectives.'

Politics

The Hashemite Kingdom of Jordan started life as the Emirate of Transjordan under Emir Abdullah in 1923 and gained independence as a monarchy in 1946 when Britain gave up its mandate. In its short but turbulent history it has survived many crises, often created by the influx of Palestinian refugees from the West Bank. These are estimated to form at least 40 per cent of the population, which has also now absorbed about half a million Iraqi refugees.

Parliamentary system

The elected Parliament amends and approves legislation initiated by the king and his government, but real power still rests with the king. Democratisation has gradually progressed and 19 political parties are registered. The last elections were in 2010 under a one-person one-vote constituency system with quotas for women and minority religious and ethnic groups. Urgent and more widespread reforms are, as of early 2011, now being demanded by protestors.

Relations with Israel

Inextricably bound up with the fates of Israel and Palestine on its borders, Jordan faces a challenging future on many fronts.

When Jordan signed its historic peace treaty with Israel in 1994, the incentives were largely economic. Huge amounts of US aid were forthcoming and the International Monetary Fund

(IMF) supervised an economic plan to straighten out the country's finances, removing subsidies which sparked food price riots. In 1999 Jordan formally renounced its sovereignty over the West Bank and East Jerusalem.

Relations with Israel go through periods of tension but are on the whole pragmatic, with the two countries agreeing in 2002 on a plan to pipe water from the Red Sea to the shrinking Dead Sea. Costing US$800 million, the project is their biggest-ever joint venture. In 2005 Jordan returned its ambassador to Israel, having withdrawn

THE PROBLEM OF ARAB UNITY

The first King Abdullah of Jordan gave a vivid description of the difficulties of Arab unity in 1945 when the Arab League was formed. It was, he said, 'a sack into which seven heads [the original seven Arab countries] had been forced, tied by ribbons of foreign domination and Arab ignorance. Such a creature could breathe, but if it attempted to move, it would choke itself to death.'

him in 2000 after the outbreak of the Palestinian uprising. Relations were strained again when King Abdullah II spoke out in the summer of 2006 against Israel and the US over the Israeli attacks on Lebanon.

Future challenges

The death of King Hussein in 1999 after 46 years of rule left an uncertain future for Jordan and its new king, Abdullah, Hussein's son by his second wife, the Englishwoman Antoinette Gardiner. Abdullah has had to grapple with the task of maintaining stability while at the same time trying to introduce political, economic and social reforms. He is helped in this task by his Palestinian wife, Rania, but the country's close links with the US are unpopular with many Jordanians, especially the Palestinian element, and implementation of the reform plans is proving tricky. The country's other problem is to restore its image as one of the region's safest destinations after well-publicised pro-democracy demonstrations and the various terrorist attacks of recent years, in which there were foreign casualties.

Politics

The Golan Heights, focus of many political wranglings in the region, tower above the River Jordan

Culture

Amman was chosen as Arab Cultural Capital by UNESCO in 2002, and its particular contribution is in the field of literature, although Jordan does also boast a handful of acclaimed modern artists. There is a thriving handicraft culture, with embroidery and jewellery-making as popular activities, encouraged by several NGOs such as the Noor Al-Hussein Foundation and Jordan River Foundation. Music and dance are a big draw at events like the Jerash Festival.

Literature

Before the 1970s very little literature emerged from Jordan, since Cairo and Beirut were the recognised centres for learning and literature in the Arab world. But in the mid-1980s the poet and artist Salma Khadra Jayyusi set up PROTA, the Project for the Translation of Arabic, which has meant that Jordanian work has started to appear in English translation, making it accessible to readers across the globe.

The indigenous Jordanian story-telling tradition was oral, based on poems sung to a musical accompaniment along with tales of tribal history. Very little of this has been translated so far, so only students of Arabic will be able to appreciate it. Palestinians, on the other hand, have a rich written literary tradition stretching back about a hundred years, so their work is better known, through writers such as Haydar Mahmoud, Mahmoud Darwish and Ibrahim Nasrallah.

Modern art

Jordan has a surprisingly vibrant modern art scene, actively promoted by Amman's Darat Al-Funun (House of Arts), which is widely regarded as one of the leading centres for contemporary art in the Arab world. It hosts lectures and film screenings, as well as housing a collection of modern Arab art.

The origins of modern art in the region are thought to go back to the 1880s under Ottoman rule, when the Ottoman army introduced compulsory drawing and topographical perspective courses for all officers. Jordan's first significant artist was one such former officer in the Ottoman army, Ziyadeen Suleyman, who staged Amman's first solo exhibition in 1938, in impressionistic style. The royal family encouraged him and other early artists, buying their work, and thereby setting a trend for wealthy families in Jordan to acquire contemporary art. After 1948 and the first Arab–Israeli war, many Palestinian artists came as refugees to

Young Jordanians wear Western-style clothing

Amman and were assimilated into the Jordanian art movement.

In the 1950s a large number of Jordanian women artists came to the fore, notably Afaf Arafat, who was the first Jordanian ever to be sent abroad to study at government expense, to Bath in England.

The 1967 Six Day War shattered all cultural developments in Jordan for several years, and many Palestinian artists emigrated to the US or Europe. By the late 1970s the art scene had recovered sufficiently for the Royal Society of Fine Arts to be set up in 1979 as a non-profit organisation. This body established Jordan's first art museum, the National Gallery of Fine Arts (*see p164*).

In the 1990s the charitable Shoman Foundation, set up by the painter Suha Shoman, inaugurated Darat Al-Funun (*see p164*), an excellent centre with exhibition space and studios. As a result, the number of galleries in Amman has boomed, helped by the purchase of local works of art by many of Jordan's leading banks and companies, seeking to decorate their headquarters and branch offices throughout the world.

Though it began as primarily impressionistic in style, contemporary Jordanian art has no specific unifying feature these days. Occasionally a few items such as Nabatean motifs might be used, but on the whole it is personal and experimental in character.

Festivals and events

In the summer, folkloric concerts and plays are held in Amman's Roman Theatre and Odeon, as well as in the towns of Salt and Fuheis, but by far the biggest cultural event in Jordan is the annual Jerash Festival.

Jerash Festival

The festival lasts nearly two months in total over July and August. Initiated by Queen Noor in 1981, it began as six days but has gradually been extended. The programme always includes a heavy dose of folk dancing in costumes, Jordanian military bands with bagpipes, Arabic plays and even such excitements as gymnasts and trapeze artists. A scantily clad Western girl hanging upside down from a high trapeze watched by women totally shrouded in black can make interesting viewing. Most of the festivities take place in Jerash's two theatres and the oval forum, but the more formal events are held at Amman's Royal Cultural Centre, with special children's events at the Haya Cultural Centre. Some events also take place at the sites of Umm Qais and Mount Nebo.

Religious festivals

The dates of Muslim religious holidays are not fixed, since their timings are dictated by the lunar calendar and therefore move backwards through the Western calendar by about 11 days each year. The Muslim calendar starts from AD 622, the date when the Prophet Muhammad and his companions fled from Mecca to Medina, where they established the first mosque. That year is given as 1 AH ('after Hijra', the 'hijra' being Muhammad's flight). Saudi Arabia is the only Arab country still to use this dating system in everyday affairs; the remainder all use the standard Gregorian system, as we do in the West.

There are two major religious festivals celebrated in all Arab

RAMADAN

Consumption of food in Ramadan, especially meat and sweets, is ironically higher than at any other time of year, as everyone makes up for the daytime abstinence by feasting after dark. Government offices and businesses have shortened hours, and efficiency is generally much impaired, not so much because of the fasting but due to lack of sleep, since the night is used for eating and celebrating.

countries. The more important one, a four-day national holiday, is called Eid Al-Adha, meaning 'Feast of the Sacrifice', which celebrates Abraham's willingness to sacrifice Isaac. The second one, a three-day national holiday, is called Eid Al-Fitr, meaning 'Feast of the Breaking of the Fast', which marks the end of Ramadan. Both holidays are celebrated with visits between family and friends, with sweets, coffee or meals being offered. Children get new clothes and often extra gifts too.

Traditional silver daggers used to be worn by men on their belts

Arab proverbs

Proverbs form a central part of Arab culture, used in everyday speech far more than in most other cultures. One scholar is said to have recorded over 4,000 of them in one small Levantine village alone. In Arabic they are not just pithy sayings but quite sophisticated, polished phrases, generally using some wordplay, alliteration, rhyme or metaphor, which are, alas, lost in translation. The following is a random selection to give the flavour and colour of these little gems to ponder over on your travels:

The well is deep…

Just like a goat, they bleat from afar and butt when they are near.

Better to ride a dung beetle than to tread on soft carpets.

The well is deep but the rope is short.

If a serpent loves thee, wear him as a necklace.

How many friends had I when my vines produced honey, how few now that they are withered.

After puberty, a husband or a grave.

Guests and fish stink after three days.

It is better to herd cattle than to rule men.

For every bean full of weevils, God supplies a blind grocer.

What camel ever saw its own hump?

Use your own brains, for no one else will lend you his.

He flies from the drain and discovers the gutter.

Who has seen tomorrow?

When I saw the mirage I threw away my water; now I have no water and no mirage.

He who makes light of other men will be killed by a turnip.

He can swallow a camel but chokes on a mosquito.

What camel ever saw its own hump?

If the turbans complain of a slight wind, what must be the state of the inner drawers?

He would burn down a city to light a cigarette.

Spit upwards and it lands on our moustache; spit downwards and it lands on our beard.

People who live on promontories know how to swim.

If you are a peg, endure the knocking; if you are a mallet, strike.

Among walnuts only the empty one speaks.

The world has not promised anything to anybody.

Lower your voice and strengthen your argument.

He who has money can eat sherbet in hell.

If life is hard on you, dwell in cities.

He makes a wine cellar from one raisin.

His brains hang at the top of his fez.

BURCKHARDT'S COLLECTION

The Anglo-Swiss explorer James Burckhardt (1784–1817) was, in 1812, the first European ever to see Petra, travelling in disguise as a Muslim pilgrim on his way to Mecca. He was sponsored by the African Association for a period of ten years to make an overland journey of discovery in the interior of Africa. He devoted the first three years to the study of Arabic and Muslim society and customs so that he could pass himself off as a local, and at the age of 25 he left England. On his travels he began collecting popular proverbial sayings. Eight years later, his body utterly exhausted from his arduous journeys, he died in Cairo. None of his work was published in his lifetime, but after his death the African Association financed the publication of his diaries, including his collection of proverbs.

Highlights

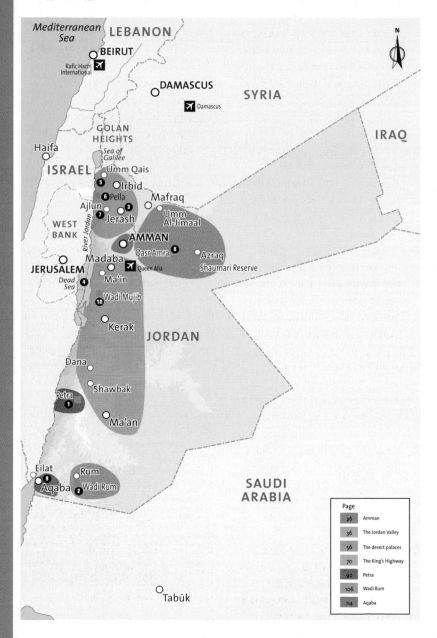

Mediterranean Sea

LEBANON

BEIRUT

Rafic Hariri International

DAMASCUS

Damascus

SYRIA

IRAQ

GOLAN HEIGHTS

Haifa

Sea of Galilee

ISRAEL

Umm Qais

5

Irbid

6 Pella

Mafraq

Ajlun

7

3

Jerash

Umm Al-Jimaal

WEST BANK

River Jordan

AMMAN

Qasr Amra **8**

Madaba

Azraq

JERUSALEM

Queen Alia

Shaumari Reserve

Dead Sea

4 Ma'in

Wadi Mujib

10

Kerak

JORDAN

Dana

Shawbak

Petra

1

Ma'an

Eilat

Rum

9

Aqaba

Wadi Rum

2

SAUDI ARABIA

Tabūk

❶ **Petra** Walking through the narrow gorge of the Siq to be confronted with the massive carved rock-face façade of the Treasury. Making the ascent to Ad-Deir, the monastery cut from the mountain. The whole site of Petra was named as one of the New Wonders of the World in 2007 (*see pp90–105*).

❷ **Wadi Rum** Camping under the stars in the magical desert mountains of Wadi Rum, and climbing to the Burdah rock bridge at dawn (*see pp106–13*).

❸ **Jerash** Strolling across the unique oval forum of this ancient Roman city and along the fine colonnaded streets worn with chariot ruts, marvelling at the carving on the temples and churches (*see pp38–41*).

❹ **The Dead Sea** Floating in the salty water 400m (1,300ft) below sea level and wallowing in the mud to treat your skin (*see pp74–5*).

❺ **Umm Qais** Exploring the ruins of this mysterious black basalt Roman site, with stunning views at sunset across the Jordan Valley to the Golan Heights (*see pp48–9*).

❻ **Pella** Sipping drinks on the terrace of the traditionally built resthouse, overlooking the ruins of the Roman city and its flowing springs in the valley below (*see pp46–7*).

❼ **Ajlun** Driving through the forested hills of northern Jordan to reach the Arab castle built by Saladin's cousin to defend against the Frankish Crusaders (*see pp44–5*).

❽ **Qasr Amra** Puzzling over the intriguing series of palaces/hunting lodges built in the desert east of Amman by the early Umayyad caliphs in the 8th century, especially Qasr Amra with its explicit murals (*see pp58–9*).

❾ **Aqaba** Enjoying the sandy beaches of Jordan's Red Sea port and admiring the marine life by diving or snorkelling around its exotic coral reefs (*see pp114–17*).

❿ **Wadi Mujib** Picnicking high up on one of the roadside vantage points overlooking this spectacular gorge that bisects the ridge of the King's Highway (*see pp80–81*).

Elaborate stonework on the Temple of Artemis, Jerash

Suggested itineraries

In an ideal world a visit to Jordan would last at least a week, though in practice, most people spend less than this, often combining it with a visit to Israel, Syria or Egypt. A really thorough visit would take two weeks, since the country is not large, and the transport network is good, with roads outside Amman relatively empty of traffic.

A 4WD is not required for any of the itineraries, except the Wadi Rum excursions where one can be hired. There is no train service in Jordan, though the bus network, known as JETT, is excellent and good value. Car hire is easy and gives you the greatest freedom in following these itineraries, though while in Amman it is simpler just to use taxis, which are ubiquitous and cheap. In the winter months, days are short, getting light at 6.30am and dark at 5pm, so this will need to be factored in when planning your itinerary. If travelling by bus, allow longer than the timings given here.

Long weekend
Day 1 Fly into Amman.
Day 2 Visit the citadel in old Amman with its Roman temples, museum and newly excavated Umayyad ruins, then north to the extensive Roman city of Jerash with its two theatres, oval forum, paved streets, temples and churches. Overnight Dead Sea.

Day 3 After swimming in the Dead Sea, drive on to Petra. Overnight Petra.
Day 4 Full day exploring Petra, requiring several hours of walking and climbing rocky paths; a good level of fitness is required.
Day 5 Return to Amman and fly home.

One week
Day 1 Fly into Amman.
Day 2 Visit Downtown Amman with its Roman amphitheatre, citadel with Roman temples and Umayyad ruins. Then travel north to the extensive Roman city of Jerash with its theatres, forum, paved streets, temples and churches. Overnight Ajlun.

The Siq at its narrowest point

Day 3 Visit the Ayyubid Arab castle built by Saladin's cousin to ward off the Crusader knights. Continue to the Roman sites of Pella and Umm Qais. Overnight Amman.

Day 4 Circuit of the desert Umayyad palaces: Qasr Al-Kharraneh, Qasr Amra, Qasr Azraq and Qasr Al-Hallabat. Overnight Amman.

Day 5 Travel down the King's Highway via the Christian mosaics of Madaba and Mount Nebo, and the Crusader castle of Kerak. Overnight Petra.

Day 6 Explore Petra for a full day on foot, a physically demanding walk with steep gradients in places. Overnight Petra.

Day 7 Excursion in Wadi Rum by camel or 4WD, continue to Aqaba for beach rest. Overnight Aqaba.

Day 8 Beach rest in the morning. Return to Amman after lunch for evening flight home.

Two weeks

Day 1 Fly into Amman.

Day 2 Explore old Downtown Amman with its Roman amphitheatre, citadel and temples, and Umayyad ruins. After lunch drive to Iraq Al-Emir in Wadi Seer, to see the Hellenistic temple. Overnight Amman.

Day 3 Drive north to the extensive Roman ruins of Jerash, then on via the Arab castle at Ajlun to the Roman site of Pella in the Jordan Valley. Overnight Pella.

Day 4 Travel up the Jordan Valley to the hilltop Roman site of Umm Qais, the springs of Mukheibeh and Al-Himmeh, and other cities of the Decapolis. Overnight Irbid.

Day 5 Drive via the black basalt caravan city of Umm Al-Jimal on to a circuit of desert Umayyad palaces, starting with Qasr Al-Hallabat, then moving on to Qasr Azraq, Qasr Amra and Qasr Al-Kharraneh. Overnight Amman.

Day 6 Start along the King's Highway via the Christian mosaics at Madaba and Mount Nebo, the hot springs at Zerqa Ma'in, Herod's Palace at Mukawir, Byzantine ruins at Umm Ar-Rasas, and Wadi Mujib. Overnight Kerak.

Day 7 Visit the Crusader castle at Kerak, then continue along the King's Highway via the Dana Wildlife Reserve and Shawbak Crusader castle. Overnight Petra.

Day 8 Whole day exploring Petra. Overnight Petra.

Day 9 Whole day at Petra and Little Petra. Overnight Petra.

Day 10 Camel or 4WD excursion in Wadi Rum. Overnight Wadi Rum.

Day 11 To Aqaba for beach rest. Overnight Aqaba.

Day 12 Dive or snorkel around Aqaba's Red Sea coral reefs. Overnight Aqaba.

Day 13 Aqaba beach rest. Overnight Aqaba.

Day 14 To Amman via the Desert Road. Overnight Amman.

Day 15 Return flight.

Amman

Anyone visiting Amman for the first time will be surprised above all by the hills. The mental image of a Middle Eastern capital set beside a river on a dusty plain must be discarded, since Amman lies on a high plateau of some 850m (2,800ft). Built originally on 7 hills, now spread on to 13 or 19 (depending on what you class as a hill), the city is dotted with a number of historic sites dating from the Stone Age to the Greek, Roman, Byzantine and Islamic eras. None is especially dramatic, but each has its own interest.

Of the hills, or *jabals* as they are known in Arabic, it is the northern and western ones which boast the prosperous and fashionable areas known as Jebel Amman, Shmeisani, Jebel Hussein and Jebel Weibdeh. Here are to be found most of the ministries, embassies, international companies and quality hotels, along with the city's middle- and upper-class residents. In the centre lies the core of the old city, known as Downtown Amman, now one

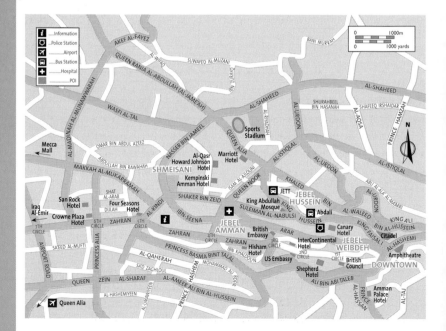

The approach to the Umayyad Palace

of the poorer areas, and to the east is the industrial sector, well located since the prevailing winds carry the industrial waste away into the desert.

When Emir Abdullah moved here in 1921 to administer the country under a British mandate, the town had a mere 3,000 inhabitants and was little more than a large village. The population of the country as a whole was 350,000, about the same as the island of Malta. Today over half the country's 6 million inhabitants live in Amman.

The city's major landmarks are the 'circles'. or roundabouts, that are simply numbered from the first upwards, and were built from this centre moving outwards as the city expanded. These days some are no longer roundabouts but are more like big junctions with traffic lights, though they are still referred to as 'circles' by everyone, especially when giving directions.

Half a day is generally considered enough to visit Amman's few historic sites, though alternatively, since Amman makes the best base for day trips to Jerash, the Dead Sea, Madaba and the desert palaces, the city sights can be slotted into the spare hour here and there between excursions.

Roman Amman

In Amman there are almost no traces of the biblical city of Rabbath-Ammon or the ancient Greek city of Philadelphia. Named after Ptolemy II Philadelphus (285–247 BC), the word in Greek means 'friend of his sister', an epithet he acquired by marrying his sister Arsinoe. What does remain today of Amman's past dates mainly from Roman times, when Emperor Trajan annexed the Nabatean kingdom with the league of ten Decapolis cities to create the Province of Arabia. Amman, situated as it was on the Roman caravan road from Bosra to Aqaba, became an important trade centre specialising in horses. It prospered, and beautiful buildings arose to reflect this prosperity: a theatre and odeum, temples and a forum.

Amphitheatre

Pictures drawn as recently as 1880 of the view from the citadel show the theatre below in isolation on a bare hillside, but today the steep slopes all around it are clustered with houses piled on top of each other. Built into the hill itself, the theatre has been meticulously restored and partially rebuilt. Dating from the 2nd century, it could hold around 6,000 spectators, and is still used for cultural performances. The area in front of the

The Roman amphitheatre in its urban setting

theatre, originally the forum, has been turned into an archaeological park, with the remains of a Corinthian colonnaded walkway and a small odeum for musical performances.

The vaulted *paradoi* of the theatre have been cleverly converted to house two attractive little museums. The **Folklore Museum**, the smaller and less interesting, contains Bedouin costumes and scenes of Bedouin daily life. The **Museum of Popular Traditions** also contains examples of Bedouin costumes but its most interesting displays are of the Bedouin jewellery in gold, silver and even Red Sea coral. A woman acquired her jewellery at marriage as part of the price the bridegroom paid to her father, and it remained entirely her own property, as a kind of insurance in the event of divorce. This system continues in Jordan today, and indeed in most Arab countries. Also of interest is the collection of stones carried by the Bedouin to cure illnesses in the belief that they had mysterious powers, worn smooth from contact with the body.

Amphitheatre and museums. Open: Sat–Thur 8am–4pm (winter), 8am–6pm (summer), Fri 10am–4pm. Admission charge.

Nymphaeum

Curiously swamped by the *souk* area of Downtown Amman (*see map p33*) stands this great hulk of a two-storey monumental fountain, dating to the 2nd century. In the 1980s the front part

The Temple of Hercules on the citadel

was occupied by shops, houses and cafés, but now the site is fenced in, awaiting restoration.
Located on Saqf Sayl (Roof of the Stream).

Temple of Hercules

Amman's only remaining temple stands up on the citadel (*see map p33*), its columns re-erected in 1993. Coins found with the head of Hercules have led experts to conclude the temple was dedicated to this god. A monumental stairway originally led from here down the hillside to the theatre, and plans are afoot to rebuild this, a project of many years.

Open: 8am–4pm. Admission charge for the whole citadel area, including the Archaeology Museum and the Umayyad Palace complex (see p32). The museum is scheduled to move into new, larger premises, although when is uncertain.

The royal family

The Kingdom of Jordan is a constitutional monarchy with the throne passing through male descent from the Hashemite dynasty of King Abdullah I (1882–1951), the son of Hussein, King of the Hejaz. The constitution itself dates from 1952, and following Abdullah's assassination in Jerusalem in 1951 the throne passed to his son Talal (1909–72), who abdicated on health grounds (possibly schizophrenia) after just one year in favour of his eldest son Hussein, then just 17 years old. Hussein's ancestry can be traced back through the Hashemite tribe directly to the Prophet Muhammad.

King Hussein

Born on 14 November 1935 and educated in Amman and then at Victoria College, Alexandria, before going on to Harrow and Sandhurst, Hussein was formally crowned king on 2 May 1953, once he had come of age and finished his schooling. In his autobiography, *Uneasy Lies the Head*, published in 1962 when he was only 27, he regrets the loss of his childhood:

King Hussein, Abdullah's father, in 1997

The price I have had to pay for position is not the unending work that I love, not the bad health that has dogged me, but a price much higher. It is that I have gone through much of my life surrounded by people, hemmed in by them, talking to them, laughing with them, envious of their casual, happy relationships, while in my heart I have been as lonely as a castaway.

Four marriages

At the age of 20 he agreed to an arranged marriage to a distant cousin, Princess Dina, by whom he had one daughter, Alia. It did not work out.

King Abdullah II

Six years later the king married a young Englishwoman, who became Princess Muna. She bore him two sons, the princes Abdullah (the current king) and Faisal, and twin daughters. Though initially happy, this marriage was also dissolved, and at the age of 37 Hussein married Alia Toukan, a Jordanian, by whom he had one daughter and one son. Queen Alia was tragically killed in a helicopter crash in 1977. One year later, aged 43, the king married the American Elizabeth Halaby, the present Queen Noor, 16 years his junior, by whom he had two sons.

Much loved by his people and widely respected on the international stage, the king died of cancer in 1999. He had nominated his son Abdullah to be Crown Prince, ignominiously removing the title from his brother Prince Hassan.

King Abdullah II

Educated in Britain and the US, Abdullah was a career soldier and once led Jordan's special forces. His glamorous wife Rania is Palestinian, and they have four children. Like Queen Noor before her, she plays an active role in social and cultural affairs in the country. Abdullah is a less charismatic character than his father, but on the whole backs political, social and economic reforms.

In early 2011 the popularity of the royal family was sorely tested by the demands for pro-democracy reforms which swept through the Arab world. Even the powerful Bedouin tribes, traditionally supporters of the king, sent letters to him in which they complained about corruption, election rigging, the non-accountability of the government and perceived political interference by Queen Rania.

Walk: Downtown Amman

The walk starts at Amman's highest point, the citadel, before taking you down to the Roman amphitheatre, then through the shops to the nymphaeum. There are no refreshments available up on the citadel, though there are cafés down near the amphitheatre.

Allow about two to three hours, including the time spent in the museum. The total distance is about 3km (2 miles).

Ask the taxi to drop you at the road entrance to the citadel site, by the ticket kiosk. After buying your ticket, which covers entry into the citadel and all it contains, walk on uphill a short way to the highest point.

1 The citadel (Al-Qal'a)

Since 1995 Spanish excavators have been carrying out extensive works on the citadel, uncovering an early 8th-century urban complex.
Walk towards the reconstructed metal dome of the Umayyad Palace, the structure which dominates the citadel.

2 Umayyad Palace/Hall

The dome was built using wood, then the metal was added. The inside is a vast hall thought to have been the vestibule of an 8th-century palace, with a few elements of decorative brickwork still remaining.
Walk on through the hall and out the other side into the colonnaded street, continuing to the edge of the citadel area.

3 The Medina

The network of excavated streets all around the Umayyad Palace/Hall gives a picture of the whole Umayyad town. Scattered about are many decorated architectural blocks, with structures that have been identified as a *souk*, a Byzantine church and an open cistern with steps down inside.
Heading towards the ticket kiosk, walk along the road to the little archaeology museum.

4 Archaeology Museum

The small museum houses a surprisingly fine collection of early artefacts, including some Dead Sea Scrolls written in Aramaic and some beautiful Byzantine jewellery.
Continue towards the ticket kiosk and fork right a little, downhill on to the wooden viewing platform.

5 Temple of Hercules

A few of the columns remain here of the Temple of Hercules (*see p29*), beyond which the wooden platform gives views down to the Roman amphitheatre below.

Exiting by the road where the taxi first dropped you off, continue down the road until you see a flight of steps leading down the hill. You emerge on to a lower road, where the steps continue in a wider form down to the very bottom. Cross the road to reach the amphitheatre, for which you'll need to buy an entrance ticket.

6 Amphitheatre

Built into the hillside in front of you is Amman's foremost Roman ruin, unusual mainly for its urban setting. After buying a ticket, you can enter, climb up the steps and also cast an eye over the two little folklore museums inside (*see p29*).

On exiting the theatre, turn left and head out of the park's landscaped area, along the main shopping street. Continue until you reach the imposing hulk of the nymphaeum.

7 Nymphaeum

This large monumental fountain is a curious relic of Roman Amman dating to the 2nd century, surrounded by streets, looking highly incongruous (*see p29*).

Catch a taxi back to your hotel.

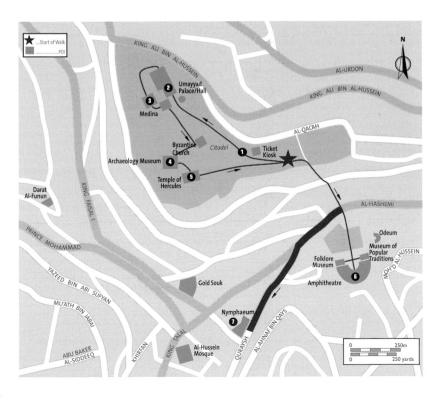

Iraq al-Emir's unique Hellenistic temple

Iraq Al-Emir

There is an interesting and short excursion to the intriguing 2nd-century BC palace at the village of Iraq Al-Emir in the Wadi As-Seer, 22km (13¹/₂ miles) west of Amman (*see map p37*). It is a unique monument, the best-preserved Hellenistic structure in the country, close to a fascinating complex of caves carved out of the cliff face. The countryside in the Wadi As-Seer is very attractive, with the little river flowing through hillsides of poplar trees, olive groves and grassy meadows. It's especially pretty in spring and makes a good picnic spot.

Practicalities

The journey takes about two hours. If you are driving, it can be incorporated at the end of a day's outing to Madaba or the Dead Sea, or at the beginning of the day, en route to Jerash.

From central Amman head for the 8th Circle and follow the signs west to Wadi As-Seer, as the road dribbles out through Amman's urban sprawl and a series of villages. The palace lies in a hollow some 10km (6¹/₄ miles) beyond the village of Wadi As-Seer, and you will know you are close when you spot the cliff face on your right with steps built up into the caves.

Open: daylight hours (the guardian lives nearby and has the key to the palace interior). Free admission.

Background

The site was first discovered in 1818, but until a joint French-Jordanian excavation project began in 1976, it had puzzled archaeologists for two centuries. Earthquakes had resulted in the collapse of the building over the centuries, and reconstruction work using cranes was finally completed in 1987. The huge palace is built of colossal limestone blocks, sometimes 6m (20ft) long by 3m (10ft) high, but only 50cm (20in) thick, and is now thought to have been surrounded by an artificial lake. With its curious mix of Egyptian concepts of scale and delicate Greek-oriental styles, it is the only monument of its kind known to exist. The protective lions carved on to the blocks were on the original floor level of the palace, to guard the royal accommodation, and the lower, smaller rooms you can enter now are thought to have been simply stores for provisions. The lion with his mouth open was a fountain, and water fed from basins inside the palace would have run out in the water channels near his paws.

Historians now generally agree that the builders of the palace were from the family of Tobias, administrator of Ammon for the Persian King Artaxerxes I in the 5th century BC. This Tobias is referred to in the Old Testament book of Nehemiah as 'the servant of Ammon', hence the palace's Arabic name Qasr Al-Abd (Palace of the Servant). The last of the Tobiads set up a small separate dynasty for himself here around 180 BC after a quarrel with the Jerusalem branch of the family, but became politically isolated and eventually took his own life.

About 700m (½ mile) before the site is a cliff face riddled with caves and a 300m (985ft)-long gallery cut into the rock, now reachable by steps, thought to have been tombs of the Tobias dynasty. The name Iraq Al-Emir means 'Caves of the Prince'.

The lions of Iraq Al-Emir were supposed to protect the palace

The Jordan Valley

The Jordan Valley is the vast geological phenomenon that forms the nothern part of the Great Rift Valley. This colossal crack in the earth's crust extends from northern Syria through the Beqaa Valley in Lebanon, into Lake Tiberias (the Sea of Galilee), then on through the Dead Sea, the Wadi Araba and the Gulf of Aqaba, all the way to East Africa 5,000km (3,100 miles) away. The valley between the Dead Sea and the Sea of Galilee is known as the Ghor, *and it is all below sea level.*

The climate of the *Ghor* is subtropical with meagre rainfall, high humidity and extremely high temperatures, especially in summer when it never drops below 38°C (100°F). The effect of this heat, closed in by the high sides of the valley and combined with the fertile alluvial soil, is of an open-air greenhouse. Crops ripen here at least two months earlier than in the surrounding countries of the Middle East, and often there are three crops a

Looking down into the Jordan Valley

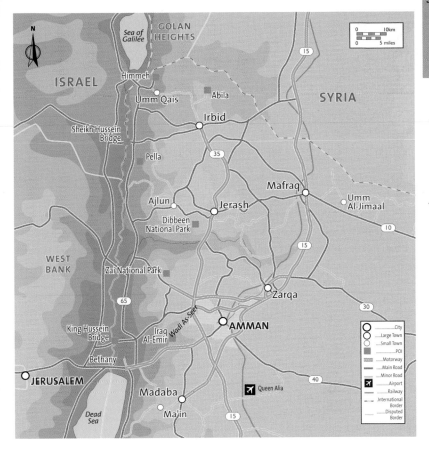

year. With the loss of the West Bank to Israel in the 1967 War, Jordan lost some 80 per cent of its fruit-growing and 45 per cent of its vegetable-growing area, so much investment was needed here to try to compensate.

The valley today, with its plastic greenhouses, concrete pipes and irrigation ditches, is a far cry from the biblical version of the Jordan, where the riverbanks were heavily wooded, the vegetation lush and abundant, and wild animals prowled the forests. The descent into the valley floor at 350m (1,150ft) below sea level from the plateau is still a spectacular one, however, from whichever point you choose to do it.

The valley has been sinking in spasmodic jerks since its formation, each jerk causing an earthquake in the area, the most recent of which was in 1927. This earthquake caused a lot of damage in Amman.

The northern end of the Cardo Maximus

Jerash

Jerash, ancient Gerasa, is one of the three great Roman sites of the Near East, the others being Petra and Palmyra (in the Syrian desert). With its magnificent colonnaded streets, its exquisite oval forum, three theatres, two temples and fifteen early Byzantine churches, it has earned the epithet 'Pompeii of the East'.

For all the excellent preservation of so many of Jerash's monuments, the area where it cannot compete with its rivals is its setting. Sprawling in a shallow valley directly on a main road, there is no gasp of amazement here to rival that first glimpse of the Treasury at Petra, no romantic enchantment as you come, after miles of endless desert, to the graceful columns of Palmyra rising against the background of the Arab castle. The ruins tumble into modern Jerash, and only in spring, when the colourful flowers help distract from the ugly town, does the setting acquire a little magic. A visit during the annual Summer Festival is recommended, as the crowds help to enhance the atmosphere of a once bustling city.

Open: 8am–4pm (winter), 8am–7pm (summer). Admission charge, in JD (local currency) only.

Excavations

When the first Western travellers stumbled on the place in the early 19th century, they found the city picturesquely abandoned in its valley, the columns tumbled, the streets heavily grassed over. In 1878 Circassian Muslim refugees from Russia were settled in the valley by the Ottoman Sultan Abdul Hamid II and took advantage of the convenient supply of stones to build their houses. Some of the eastern part of Roman Jerash disappeared under what is now the modern town, and excavation works have continued on and off throughout the 20th century, carried out by the British, Germans, Americans and the Jordanian Department of Antiquities. The Germans did especially well, finding in 1907 a superb Roman mosaic with mythological scenes, the finest mosaic ever found in Jerash. It was shipped to Germany and, after more than 50 years locked up in the storerooms of Berlin's Pergamon Museum, it is now on display there.

Roman wealth

Although there was a Hellenistic city here as early as the 4th century BC, everything extant in Jerash today dates from Roman times. Gerasa was captured by the Roman Empire in 84 BC, and Pompey, in carving up the territory into provinces, put it into the province of Syria. In practice it governed itself to a large extent, and then joined the Decapolis, a league of ten free cities. Trade and agriculture flourished under the Pax Romana, and by the 2nd century AD the city had amassed so much wealth that it was virtually able to rebuild itself as we see it today. The city walls are still traceable for most of their 3.5km (2-mile) length and enclose the city in a rough circle. The Roman population was estimated at about 15,000. The Ionic columns of the oval forum were thought originally to have been painted in reds, yellows, blues and greens. The Cardo Maximus had 260 Corinthian columns along either side, and the chariot wheel ruts are still clear, worn into the original stone paving.

The Jordan Valley

Hadrian's Gate marks the southern end of Jerash

Walk: Around Jerash

Apart from any clambering up the steps of the theatre and other buildings, this site is on the flat, but good footwear is essential to cope with the uneven stones. Shade is scarce, so time your visit carefully to avoid the midday sun in the hotter months. The site's resthouse makes a welcome break for refreshments. There are toilets at the entrance.

After buying your entrance ticket, follow the dirt track a short way to Hadrian's Gate, the starting point of the walk.

The walk is about 3km (2 miles). Allow at least two hours.

1 Hadrian's Gate

This splendid triumphal arch was built in AD 129 in honour of Emperor Hadrian's visit. Its three vaulted passageways mark the beginning of the old road that led to the city's main South Gate. The theatres, temples, forum and baths all date from this time, when the region benefited from the prosperity and stability of Rome. *Walk on from the arch, passing the hippodrome on your left (where chariot races are now enacted), to reach the resthouse and South Gate where you enter the site proper.*

2 Oval Forum

This jewel of Jerash is the first thing you will see as the path opens up. Its beautiful shape has led to speculation that it may have been a place of sacrifice for the Temple of Zeus above, rather than the actual market place.

After exploring the Temple of Zeus and the theatre, walk out of the forum along the Cardo Maximus, passing the little museum on your right, over the first crossroads and on until you reach the cathedral after about 400m (¼ mile).

3 Cathedral

Approached up a wide stairway, the cathedral was built in the mid-4th century AD. Jerash at its height boasted 15 churches, and the main ones are visitable in a cluster here behind the cathedral.
Follow the path through the Fountain Court to reach the Church of St Theodore.

4 Churches

Keep an eye out for mosaics on the floors of the churches, the finest of which are in the Church of Sts Cosmos and Damian, viewable over the high wall. There are also fragments in the Church of St George and the Church of John the Baptist.

*Head back towards the Church of
St Theodore, then fork left up a path
on to the huge platform of the Temple
of Artemis.*

5 Temple of Artemis

This is the most impressive of all
Jerash's buildings in its sheer scale
and power, as befits the patron
goddess of the city. The temple
forms the core of an elaborately
planned series of stairways, gateways
and courtyards.

*Exit the temple at the highest point,
heading towards the north theatre, from
which point the walk is all downhill.
Return to the Cardo Maximus,
passing the propylaeum (entrance)
of the temple, to reach the nymphaeum
on the right.*

6 Nymphaeum

The two-storey monumental façade of
the fountain is elaborately decorated,
with a fine huge stone basin.
Walk back to the ticket office.

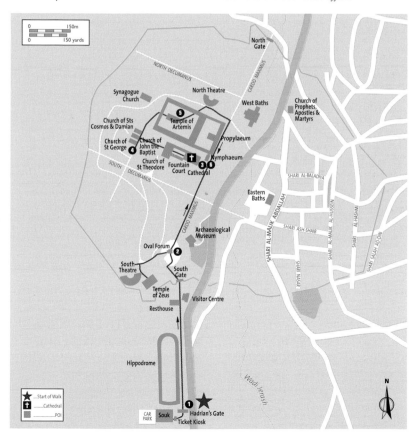

Early Christianity

Christianity became the state religion of the Roman Empire in 324 when Emperor Constantine announced his own conversion. With its doctrine of equality for all souls, the new religion had instant appeal, and six years later Constantine founded a new Christian imperial capital which he named after himself. Constantinople, in the ancient Greek colony of Byzantium, is today's Istanbul. This marked the beginning of the split between the Eastern and Western churches, between Rome and Constantinople, later formalised in 395.

Pilgrimages

Constantine's mother, Helena, established a trend by making a pilgrimage to Jerusalem in 326. The first church in Jordan was built at much the same time on Mount Nebo to commemorate Moses' death. As the rate of pilgrimages increased, the area around Mount Nebo and the nearby town of Madaba gradually developed into a focus for pilgrimage. By the end of the 4th century a large number of churches had been built in the area, often on the foundations of Roman temples and often featuring fine mosaic floors.

Rise and fall

Eastern Christians were split between about a dozen sects, supposedly on doctrinal differences over the 'nature' of Christ – human or divine – but in reality representing more of a desire for independence from Constantinople among the populations of the provinces in the 4th and 5th centuries.

MOSAICS

Jordan has a fine tradition of mosaic flooring. The earliest example, dating to the 1st century BC, was from Herod's Palace at Mukawir and is now on display in the Madaba museum. The latest ones date from the 8th century when Christian mosaicists were still permitted to work under the Muslim caliphate. In secular buildings like palaces, public baths and private villas, the preference was for classical scenes from Greek and Roman mythology. In churches the favoured motifs were the Christian symbols of the fish and the lamb, and personifications of the earth, sea and seasons. Biblical scenes also served as pictorial aids to teach the Bible in an age where only a tiny group of elite would have been able to read it. Many of the mosaics depicting people suffered damage when the Umayyad Caliph Yazid II (719–24) declared that representation of humans, and by extension animals, was blasphemous as only God could 'create' living creatures. Yet more damage was done to the mosaics during the iconoclastic period after 726 when Emperor Leo III banned the use of icons in worship.

Plague, wars against the Persian Sassanians and doctrinal infighting weakened the Byzantine Empire in the Levant during the 6th and early 7th centuries to such an extent that it took only ten years for the Muslim armies to dismantle it, which they finally achieved in 636.

Christianity in Jordan today

Today Christians form just 10 per cent of the Syrian population and 6 per cent of the Jordanian, but their influence in the region is far greater than these figures might suggest, because of their economic power and their important links to the West. The Greek Orthodox form the majority, about two thirds, though there are also Greek Catholics (known in Jordan as Latin), and small numbers of Protestants. Most continue to be clustered in the areas round Madaba, Salt, Fuheis, Kerak, Ajlun and Amman. They follow the Christian pattern of closing their shops on Sundays instead of Fridays.

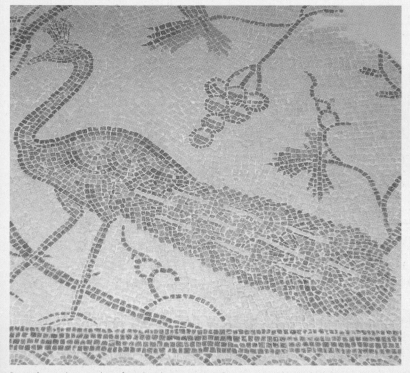

Peacock mosaic at Jordan's first church on Mount Nebo

Qalaat Ar-Rabadh, Ajlun

Perched on its hilltop in solitary splendour among the forests of northern Jordan is this rare example of a true Arab castle, Qalaat Ar-Rabadh. From its vantage point there are excellent views to the west and the hills of distant Judea, and even Jerusalem is said to be visible on a clear day. In high summer the castle, with its cool breezes, is a popular outing for Gulf families holidaying in Jordan.

The upper part of Ajlun still has a Christian community with two churches, and the mosque to the left of the castle approach road is thought, from its square 13th-century minaret, to have been converted from a Byzantine church.

Bridge across the moat at Qalaat Ar-Rabadh

Practicalities

A tarmac road now leads from the town of Ajlun right up to the parking area in front of the castle, with a few souvenir shops, refreshment stalls and toilets. *25km (15¹/₂ miles) north of Jerash (half an hour's drive). Open: 8am–4pm (winter), 8am–7pm (summer). Admission charge.*

Treacherous beginnings

Built in 1184 by the Ayyubid Emir Izz Ad-Din Osama, a cousin of Saladin and one of his most able governors, the castle's chief purpose was to guard the western border of Ayyubid territory. Its secondary role was as a defence against the feuding local emirs, and when they queried his project, Osama pretended he was building it as protection against the Crusaders who were already installed in the Emirs' castles at Kerak and Shawbak. This satisfied them and they even helped him build it. When it was finished Osama invited them to a celebratory banquet, and, after they had eaten their fill, he had them all locked up to try out the new dungeons.

More peaceful times

Most of the present castle dates from Saladin's time; the oldest parts are recognisable by the coarser, heavier stonework and the narrower window or arrow slits. The 13th-century Mameluke additions are more finely crafted and have wider windows, reflecting the castle's changed role to a more administrative function. In

Qalaat Ar-Rabadh is surrounded by forest

Mameluke times the castle was one of a chain of points that linked Damascus to Cairo by pigeon post, a system which enabled the Sultan in Cairo to hear news of events on his northern borders the same day. The castle was unfortunate enough to be in the way of the Mongol hordes in 1260, but though they plundered it, they caused less damage than the earthquake of 1837, which left it collapsing and dangerous.

The castle today

Despite its superb position, the slopes surrounding it are not especially steep, and so to protect it further from attack, a deep dry moat was dug. In the 1960s the entrance could only be reached by climbing up iron rungs embedded in the rock, but today, as would have been the case originally, a wooden drawbridge has been built to span the wide gully. Inside, the stone-vaulted corridor kinks first right, then left to enter the castle through its original gate. Stairways, passages and doorways lead off tantalisingly in all directions to a multitude of different levels, usually leading eventually to one of the towers.

The Roman remains at Pella

Pella

Tucked up in an eastern side valley of the Jordan Valley, the ruins of Pella are among the most attractively situated of any of Jordan's ancient Roman cities.

Practicalities

Locally the site is known as Tabaqat Al-Fahl, and is signposted as such from the main road that runs along the valley floor. The approach road forks uphill through a scruffy town, to emerge after about 1km (²/3 mile) at the entrance to the fenced ruins. Alternatively, you can continue uphill for another 2km (1¹/4 miles) to fork right at the charming resthouse, whose terrace has superb views westwards over the site;

the food and refreshments on offer here are excellent. Since the ruins are very spread out, the considerable amount of walking involved in a tour of the site requires a good intake of sustenance.

Open: 8am–6pm. Free admission via the resthouse.

Setting

From the resthouse terrace you can also digest the history of the place, all 7,000 years of it, starting from neolithic times. The site always appealed due to its natural advantages, spared the worst of the heat by being located on a side valley, sheltered from the sharp frosts and cold winter winds of the highland plateau, and with its own spring, Ain Al-Jirm, which has water even in the hottest months. According to Egyptian papyri of 1250–1000 BC, Pella had around 5,000 inhabitants, and produced the wooden spokes for the chariot wheels of Pharaonic Egypt, a fact which shows that the bare hills you see today were not always so.

Greek, Roman and Byzantine times

It became a real city when it was founded by former generals of Alexander the Great's army, who named it Pella after the town in Macedonia where Alexander was born. The Hellenistic town was destroyed around 80 BC by Israelite troops because the inhabitants would not promise to adopt Jewish customs. After the Roman conquest in 64 BC, Pella was rebuilt and became one of the cities of the Decapolis league. In the Christian era it was a thriving town with its own bishop, and enjoyed its heyday during the Byzantine era in the 4th century when it was much visited as a spa.

Pella's most impressive monument, the colossal Great Basilica, also dates from that time, its monumental stairway leading to the west towards the spring. During the 5th and 6th centuries Pella was heavily populated and the slopes of the surrounding hills were all covered in houses, the remains of which can still be seen in parts.

Battles and earthquakes

An important battle took place here in 635 between the Arabs and a strong Byzantine army, in which the Byzantines were roundly defeated and a staggering total of 80,000 Greeks were said to have been killed. It was known thereafter by the Arabs as the Battle of the Fahl (Marsh), as the Byzantines had broken the nearby dams. This is also where it gets its current name, Tabaqat Al-Fahl (Terraces of the Marsh). Three earthquakes, in 658, 717 and 747, destroyed most of the buildings and killed many of the inhabitants, and human bones have been found under some of the blocks during excavations.

The ancient columns still stand tall at Pella

Umm Qais

The location of this Graeco-Roman city right up in the extreme northwest corner of the country, on the crest of a hill facing out towards the Sea of Galilee and the Golan Heights, is the most spectacular of any in Jordan. The view from the superb terrace of its resthouse is, on a clear day at sunset, arguably the finest in the country.

Practicalities

The resthouse has a craft shop and serves excellent food.
Two hours' drive from Amman.
Open: 8am–sunset. Admission charge.

Biblical links

Known in biblical times as Gadara, it is thought to have been here that Christ made himself unpopular by

The basalt columns of Umm Qais have been restored

transferring the unclean spirits from two wild men to a herd of Gadarene swine: 'And behold, the whole herd of swine ran violently down a steep place into the sea, and perished in the waters...' (Matthew 8:28).

Two tombs with colossal limestone doors carved to resemble fortified metal, and wooden doors with Greek inscriptions above the lintels, can still be seen on the site. These may be the very tombs from which the two men were said to have emerged before meeting Jesus. The doors still swing on their stone hinges and were, fittingly, in use until recently as goat pens.

Literature and leisure

As a Graeco-Roman settlement and one of the most important towns of the Decapolis, Gadara prided itself on its cultural life. It produced a succession of famous philosophers and poets, the best known of whom was a 2nd-century satirist and poet called Meleager, who was Phoenician by origin, and known especially for his epigrams: 'Island Tyre was my nurse, and Gadara, which is Attic, but lies in Syria, gave birth to me... If I am Syrian, what wonder? Stranger, we dwell in one country, the world; One Chaos gave birth to all mortals.'

The inhabitants of Gadara also took their leisure seriously, enjoying the hot springs below in El-Himmeh. Strabo wrote: 'To Gadara the pleasure-loving Romans, after having enjoyed the restorative effects of the hot springs

The main street at Umm Qais

down in the valley, retired for refreshment, enjoying the cooler heights of the city and solacing their leisure with the plays performed in the theatres.'

Excavations and restorations

German excavations have, since 1977, gradually transformed the site, which was previously just a jumble of stones inhabited by a few Bedouin families. Several earthquakes, particularly the one in 747, inflicted great damage, leaving much of the city in ruins. Over the years, the German team has re-erected the impressive black basalt Corinthian columns of the main Byzantine church of the city, and restored the two theatres; the smaller West Theatre is especially fine, with its vaulted tunnel in Roman style still running intact round the semicircle under the black basalt blocks that form the seats.

From the 4th to the 7th centuries the town was an episcopal seat of some importance, and the floor of the elegant main basilica is decorated with marble and geometric patterns. Above the basilica on the rocky outcrop are the resthouse and a cluster of Turkish Ottoman houses which the archaeologists used as their accommodation. One of these is now a museum and several have been restored.

Drive: Cities of the Decapolis

This unusual and interesting two-day drive takes you on a tour around Jordan's most scenic countryside, through the forested hills and valleys of the northwest, exploring several of the Decapolis sites, a wealthy confederation of Graeco-Roman cities.

The round trip is about 300km (186 miles).

Set off from Amman, and drive around 45km (28 miles) north to Jerash.

1 Jerash

Explore the extensive ruins of ancient Gerasa, the most famous of the Decapolis cities (*see pp38–9*). Have lunch at the resthouse within the site. *Drive on 23km (14 miles) through the tree-covered hills to reach Ajlun, then follow the signs a further 3km (2 miles) to Qalaat Ar-Rabadh.*

2 Qalaat Ar-Rabadh

Visit the hilltop Arab castle, built in Crusader times and still in fine condition (*see pp44–5*).
Return to Ajlun then follow the road west as it descends into the Jordan Valley, dramatically dropping off the high plateau to 400m (1,300ft) below sea level. Turn right (north) at the bottom to reach Pella after 23km (14 miles).

3 Pella (Tabaqat Al-Fahl)

Arrive late afternoon with time to explore the picturesque ruins among the springs before dining

in the resthouse and staying in the charming guesthouse (*see pp46–7*). *Drive on north through the Jordan Valley, reaching a checkpoint after about 25km (15¹⁄₂ miles), where the road starts to head up towards the Golan Heights of Syria, occupied by Israel since 1973. No photos may be taken in this heavily militarised zone, but the scenery is stunning, with the gorge of the Yarmuk River below, visible throughout the final 15km (9-mile) approach to Umm Qais.*

4 Umm Qais (Gadara)

Take your time exploring the two theatres, basilicas, baths and tombs of this spectacularly sited city, before enjoying lunch on the terrace of the resthouse within the site (*see pp48–9*). *Continue on the road to Irbid until you reach a turn-off left to Wadi El-Queilbeh and Horta, about 7km (4 miles) before Irbid. Head north for another 7km (4 miles) until you cross at right angles a valley with a spring to the left of the road. From here a dirt track leads over the hill to the west of the wadi, and this will take you to the ruins of Abila.*

5 Abila

Yet to be excavated and charmingly rural, the site of Abila has the remains of a theatre and a basilica. In the wadi itself are several hundred Roman tombs, 20 with frescoes, built into the cliffs (*see p52*).

Return to the main road and continue to the village of Beit Ra's, 5km (3 miles) north of Irbid.

6 Beit Ra's and Capitolias

Built into the houses and scattered in the gardens and yards of the village known today as Beit Ra's, you will find the visible ruins of the ancient city of Capitolias: old stone blocks and carved capitals (the decorated tops of temple columns). A major tomb lies under the playground of the village school.

Continue into Irbid and follow the road straight down through Jerash, returning to Amman by sundown.

Drive: Cities of the Decapolis

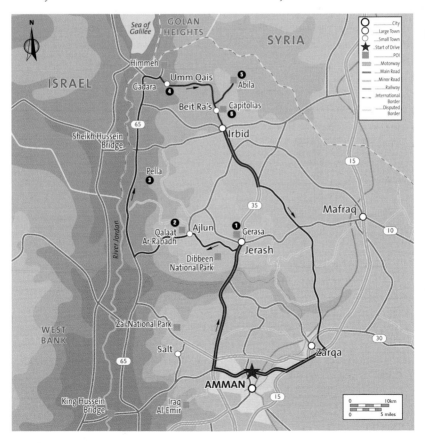

Irbid, Abila, Himmeh and Umm Al-Jimaal

These places are clustered in Jordan's northwest corner and are not often visited, as they lie a little off the beaten track.

Irbid

Irbid is Jordan's major town of the north, lying some 70km (43 miles) north of Amman, and the country's chief agricultural and industrial centre, with one of the fastest-growing populations in the country. This growth has left Irbid itself a town of neither character nor charm but of endless half-finished streets and buildings. In 1976 the new Yarmouk University was set up here with Saudi money, and the vast campus on the edge of town is one of the few landmarks.

Northwest Jordan, near Himmeh

The collection comprising the **Museum of Jordanian Heritage** (*open: Sat–Wed 10am–5pm; free admission*), housed within Yarmouk University, is small, yet possibly the best historical and archaeological museum in the country, superbly and clearly laid out. It merits a visit of a good hour, and will help put all periods of Jordan's history into a clear context, with carefully chosen high-quality exhibits.

Abila

Set in the Wadi El-Queilbeh just a few kilometres north of Irbid are the bucolic remains of Abila, one of the Decapolis cities that remains unexcavated, picturesquely abandoned in the fields, its theatre and basilica a jumbled heap of stones. Of special interest is its necropolis, a series of tombs cut into the cliffs of the nearby wadi, some of them with colourful frescoes inside. A torch will be required for proper exploration, and a visit is not recommended for anyone suffering from arachnophobia or claustrophobia.

Himmeh

In Roman times the exotic baths complex of Gadara, now Umm Qais, was centred on the seven hot springs here. Most of the Roman remains now lie within what is known as Syrian Himmeh, on the north bank of the Yarmouk and now in Israeli-occupied territory, just 5km (3 miles) north of Umm Qais. Jordanian Himmeh, also known as Mukheibeh, 200m (656ft) below sea level, boasts only a rather fetid but large pool, part of Al-Hameh Restaurant and Recreation, which has two-hour alternating shifts for men and women. Women are not advised to bathe here in the warm sulphurous water in anything less than a T-shirt and long shorts.

Open: 6am–8pm. Admission charge.

Umm Al-Jimaal

This rarely visited Byzantine ghost town lies just 50km (31 miles) east of Jerash, not far from the Syrian border, and can be visited in half a day from Amman, Irbid or Ajlun. To reach it you must follow signs beyond Mafraq towards Iraq and Baghdad. At first the sprawling black ruins look like a burnt or bombed city. In the absence of trees, no wood was used in the construction of the buildings; everything was made from the black basalt that was spat out in lava streams all over this area of northern Jordan and southern Syria desert by the volcanoes of the Jebel Druze in Syria. As a result the buildings are unusually well preserved, often still retaining their ceilings and upper storeys. Umm Al-Jimaal is thus one of the best examples of a small Christian Byzantine city ever built on the edge of a Muslim Arab empire, complete with 15 churches, a cathedral, houses and administrative buildings. Remarkable, too, is its elaborate water system of cisterns and aqueducts, a tribute to the ingenuity of the people in a region devoid of natural springs.

Open: daylight hours. Free admission.

The remains of Umm Al-Jimaal

Al-Maghtas, where Jesus Christ was baptised

Bethany

The identification of this site, sometimes called 'Bethany-beyond-the-Jordan', has been the most important archaeological discovery in the Middle East in recent years. Also known as Al-Maghtas (Baptism Site), it has now been authenticated as the place where John the Baptist lived and where he baptised Jesus Christ. It fell within a military zone in 1967 and was subsequently out of bounds for many years. Only after the 1994 peace treaty with Israel was it accessible again and archaeologists, using pre-1948 studies, were able to identify 21 separate sites along the Wadi Kharrar, a small side valley that runs from its source some 2km (1¼ miles) down into the River Jordan.

They found eleven Byzantine churches, five baptismal pools dating from Roman and Byzantine times, pilgrims' lodgings and many monks' and hermits' caves. On the strength of all this evidence the site was internationally recognised, and in March 2000 Pope John Paul II came to celebrate open-air Mass with 25,000 worshippers.

Practicalities

On arrival at the site, all vehicles must be parked at the entrance, in one of three car parks: Parking 1 beside Elijah's Hill, Parking 2 beside the Pilgrims' Station, and Parking 3 by the Church of John the Baptist. Toilet facilities are at Parkings 2 and 3 and the Visitor Centre. The latter has simple refreshments and drinks and there are water fountains provided along the pathways.

After buying your ticket you get a free brochure with a map and park at the Visitor Centre, from where the free shuttle buses run every 15–20 minutes to the three main areas of the site, spread over 6sq km (2⅓ sq miles). About three hours should be allowed for a full visit. By keeping cars at a distance, the Jordanian authorities have succeeded in retaining the special atmosphere of the site.
The site is signposted off the main Amman–Dead Sea highway and lies 5km (3 miles) from the Dead Sea junction.

Open: 8am–5pm (Nov–Mar), 8am–6pm (Apr–Oct), last entry one hour before closing. Admission charge includes shuttle bus and a 60-minute guided tour.

Church of John the Baptist

The walk from Parking 3 brings you into a heavily vegetated, almost jungle area, in the middle of which stands this 6th-century church, alongside two more, built one on top of the other. This spot, with 14 gurgling springs and the tumbled marble capitals of antiquity, is possibly the most atmospheric of all.

The Pilgrims' Station

Heading downhill 500m (⅓ mile) to the west from Parking 3 is a complex of hermits' cells, and further still, near Parking 2, is a baptismal pool fed by spring waters, large enough to accommodate 300 people. Above it on a promontory is a 5th-century building thought to have been a hostel for visiting pilgrims. On the other side of the Wadi Kharrar, modern steps lead to two caves with prayer niches and apses.

Tell Mar Elias

The Pope celebrated his open-air Mass here beneath the commemorative arch built in memory of King Hussein. There are three churches, three caves and three baptismal pools viewable from a wooden catwalk. Fragmentary mosaics are also visible, and the spot is said to be where Elijah rose into heaven.

The desert palaces

The desert palaces have always excited controversy as to their exact purpose and role. There are over 20 of them scattered around Lebanon, Syria, Israel and Jordan, always in solitary locations, and showing a variety of confusing architectural patterns.

Jordan can boast the best and most readily accessible examples of these desert palaces. Sometimes they resemble Roman-Byzantine castles like Qasr Al-Kharraneh, sometimes Syrian-Byzantine baths like Qasr Amra, sometimes Parthian-Sassanid halls or

caravanserais with four vaulted niches on each side, like Qasr Azraq. The confusion is compounded by the fact that the builders frequently used existing buildings which they adapted to their purposes. As a result the palaces have been variously dated to AD 293,

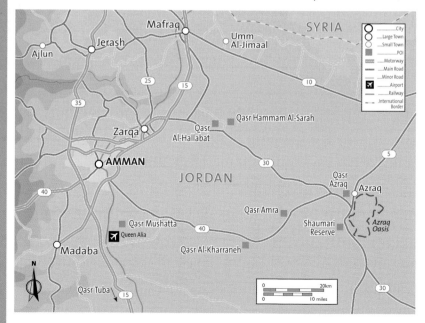

Interior courtyard of Qasr Al-Kharraneh

the 4th and 6th centuries, and to the
Umayyad period in the 8th century.

Apart from any defensive function, it
is clear, especially from Qasr Amra, that
the palaces' other chief purpose was as
weekend getaways from the worries and
strains of state. They were places where
wine, women and song induced
relaxation and where much poetry,
notably love poetry, was written. The
following is an example that has
survived from the 8th century:

*Ah for the throes of a heart sorely
wounded!*

*Ah for the eyes that have smitten me
with madness!*
*Gently she moved in the calmness of
beauty,*
*Moved as the bough to the light breeze
of morning.*
*Dazzled my eyes as they gazed, till
before me*
All was a mist and confusion of figures.
*Ne'er had I sought her, and ne'er had
she sought me;*
*Fated the hour, and the love, and the
meeting.*

Omar Ibn Abi Rabi'a, died 720

QASR AMRA

Always thought of as the high point of any tour of the desert palaces, Qasr Amra stands out as unique, thanks to its extraordinary frescoes, which in their isolated location escaped the attentions and destruction of the iconoclasts.

Practicalities

The new layout and Visitor Centre mean you now have to approach this tiny but charming pleasure palace from the hill above, the path winding down a short distance to reach it. Flash photography is permitted inside, surprisingly.
Open: 7am–7.30pm (summer), 8am–4.30pm (winter). Admission charge includes Qasr Azraq and Qasr Al-Kharraneh (see pp62–3 & 66–7).

A dancing girl on a fresco

JUDGEMENT OF THE IMAGE MAKERS

According to the strict Islamic view, the representation of human or animal forms in art is the prerogative of Allah alone. The basis for this ban on subject matter lies not in the Koran, but in a quote from the Prophet Muhammad that on the Day of Judgement, the most severely punished would be the 'portrayers' or 'image makers'. Strict subsequent interpretation of this passage has meant that no human representation is to be found in any mosque, and almost all the decorative motifs throughout the Muslim world derive from plants or abstract geometric patterns.

Frescoes

The lavish frescoes decorating Qasr Amra's baths are the best-preserved examples of Umayyad painting in the world, which is why they have been awarded UNESCO World Heritage status. However, their interest lies not only in their excellent state of preservation, but also in the content. Contrary to the strict Islamic view of appropriate subject matter, here at Qasr Amra the early Muslims had paintings of naked women bathing, scenes of frolicking and dancing, hunting scenes with men and dogs chasing gazelles into nets, men on foot spearing horses, bears playing lutes, and camels and horses working in the fields.

The palace was built between 711 and 715, making it the earliest example yet known of Muslim picture art. The pleasure-loving Al-Walid I was the builder, choosing scenes that gave him greatest enjoyment. On the right-hand

The desert setting of Qasr Amra

wall on entry, beyond the large painting of the woman rising from the bath, is a curious though damaged scene of six kings conquered by the Umayyads, with their names underneath in Greek and Kufic Arabic script. It is said to be an illustration of a poem by Yazid III on the family of the kings of the world.

AL-WALID I

Al-Walid I died at the age of 40, but during his pleasure-packed life he had some of the finest Umayyad constructions built. He enlarged the beautiful great mosque at Mecca, and rebuilt that of Medina. In Syria he built many schools, mosques and hospitals for the poor and the infirm. In Jerusalem he put the gilded brass dome on the Dome of the Rock, lifted from a church in Baalbek, Lebanon. In Damascus he converted the site of the Cathedral of John the Baptist into the Great Umayyad Mosque, still today the fourth-holiest mosque in Islam after Mecca, Medina and Jerusalem.

Graffiti

Some restoration work was carried out in the 1970s by a Spanish team, for over the years the frescoes acquired their fair share of graffiti. Their reputation for being haunted is thought to have spared them to some extent. More recent vandalism is attributed to the army. The colours, shielded from light by the virtual absence of windows, have remained rich, with reds, greens, browns and blues.

Early Islam: the Umayyads

The Umayyads, under their leader Mu'awiya, were the first settled dynasty of caliphs in Islam. The Bedouin horsemen surging out of the Arabian Peninsula had conquered Egypt and all of the Levant at remarkable speed. After the Prophet Muhammad's sudden death in 632, his followers had acquired a new empire which now needed to be administered. First they had to establish a base, and in 661 they founded their new capital at Damascus, which was to be the centre of the empire for the next two centuries.

People of the desert
As simple tribesmen suddenly in charge of a huge machine, with all its attendant ties and responsibilities, it was not unnatural for them to long for the sporting life of the desert that was in their bones and had been integral to their upbringing. Sometimes this longing for the old days was channelled into such exploits as raiding and looting the southern coastal towns of Turkey, where they left a trail of destruction throughout the 7th and 8th centuries. On other occasions it took a more harmless form: the building of fantasy palaces in the desert. There they could escape the cares of government and administration, and enjoy instead the pursuits of hawking, camel racing, wine, women, music and poetry – all the traditional Arab pleasures in their natural setting. The palaces were never really castles, as any defensive function they may sometimes have had was always secondary to their primary purpose – the pursuit of pleasure.

The good life
From the late 7th century onwards the tradition continued, and later Umayyad caliphs, notably Abd Al-Malik and Walid II, built their country

MU'AWIYA AND HIS FAMILY

Supreme organiser that he was, Mu'awiya laid the foundations of a stable, orderly society after becoming caliph in 661. He was the first to introduce a registry system for recording the affairs of state, and he began the first proper postal system, using relays of horses. Yet from among his many wives, he chose as his favourite a Jacobite Christian called Maysun. Of Bedouin origins, she abhorred the rigid court life of Damascus and longed for the freedom of the desert. She used to take their son Yazid to the desert where they would roam with her tribesfolk, and where the young prince acquired a taste for hard riding, hunting, drinking wine and composing poetry.

The Umayyad Palace/Hall in Amman

residences in the desert and called them *Badiyahs*. Their pure Arabic language escaped the corruptions of Aramaic and other foreign elements, and they also avoided the infectious plagues that afflicted the cities of Syria at regular intervals. Here in the desert each prince received what was held to be the perfect education; he learned to read and write Arabic, to use the bow and arrow and to swim, and he acquired the ethical ideals of courage, endurance of hardship, manliness, generosity and hospitality, regard for women and the keeping of promises. After all this he would be termed '*al-kaamil*' (the perfect one). Occasionally things did not go so smoothly, and when the Caliph Hisham's young son was killed in a fall from his horse while hunting, his father commented wryly: 'I brought him up for the caliphate and he pursues a fox!'

QASR AZRAQ AND QASR AL-HALLABAT

These two desert castles are defensive in role and architecture, resembling forts far more than palaces.

Qasr Azraq

The Azraq oasis is no great beauty spot, and though there are palm trees, the sprawling, half-finished modern constructions all around detract from any charm the place may once have had.

The black basalt fort here at the roadside in the northern part of town

was originally of Roman construction and built in the 3rd century. Attracted by the rich hunting to be found in the oasis, with lions, lynx, gazelles and antelopes, the Umayyad Caliph Walid II came here in the 8th century.

Today the most important thing in the fort has become the room over the gatehouse reached by outside steps, where T E Lawrence stayed for a month after arriving from Aqaba and Wadi Rum. There he waited for all the tribal armies of the Arab Revolt to congregate

The bath works at Hammam Al-Sarah

before their final assault on Damascus in 1918 (*see pp12–13*).

Open: daylight hours. Admission included in the same ticket as Qasr Amra and Qasr Al-Kharraneh (see pp58–9 & 66–7).

Shaumari Wildlife Reserve

Around 15km (9 miles) to the south of the fort, this modest reserve is popular with school outings. It has successfully reintroduced the oryx, now extinct in the Jordanian desert, and also boasts ostriches and gazelles.
Open: 9am–sunset. Admission charge.

Qasr Al-Hallabat

The palace was originally a Roman fortress, probably built under Marcus Aurelius to control the northeastern edge and to protect it against Parthian attacks from the east. This defensive function is clearly recognisable even now, not only from its raised position, but also from its high, thick outer walls built in a square and defended by towers at the corners. In 529 Emperor Justinian renovated the castle, and for a short period in the 7th century Christian monks used it as a monastery. The Umayyad princes took it over at the beginning of the 8th century and decorated it more in the style of a palace, with elaborate tiled marble flooring in geometric patterns and carved frescoes.

Many of the stones used in construction have Nabatean Greek and Latin inscriptions, and were probably

brought from nearby Byzantine sites like Umm Al-Jimaal. Stairways lead up to the second storey, and in many of the rooms there are finely worked mosaics of animals such as lions, bulls, ostriches, bearded serpents and wildfowl, framed by foliage and a geometric edging. Before restoration many were covered with a protective layer of soft mortar. The other striking feature in the building is the contrast between the sandy-coloured limestone blocks and the black basalt ones.

Immediately in front of the palace the small building with three gateways is an Umayyad mosque. The Umayyads also constructed a complex water system with dams, cisterns and water channels on the edge of a wadi to supply the palace.

The new fencing, car park and Visitor Centre requires that you walk 400m (1/4 mile) up the hillock to view Qasr Al-Hallabat.
Open: daylight hours. Admission charge includes Hammam Al-Sarah (see below).

Hammam Al-Sarah

Standing by itself 2km (1 1/4 miles) before the palace is this tiny hunting pavilion built around a set of small baths. It was erected in 725. At the beginning of the 20th century, early European visitors could still see traces of coloured frescoes on the bath walls, but these have since disappeared.
Open: daylight hours. Admission included with Qasr Al-Hallabat ticket.

Drive: Desert palaces

A circuit of the palaces of the Umayyad caliphs, which lie strung out in the desert east of Amman, is one of the highlights of a trip to Jordan, a very enjoyable and instructive sortie into a rarely seen side of early Islam. Now that they are linked by a new tarmac road, the main ones can easily be visited in a day trip from Amman.

The total round trip is 260km (160 miles).

Combine a day trip with lunch and perhaps a swim at Azraq or, to look more closely and include the Byzantine caravan city of Umm Al-Jimaal, stay overnight at the Azraq Eco-lodge (see p167) and enjoy the Chechen cuisine and hospitality.

Head south from Amman on the airport road, then fork left towards Azraq through the industrial sprawl on the eastern outskirts of the city, following signs to Iraq, Saudi Arabia and Azraq. The first palace lies on this road after 65km (40 miles), just off to the right.

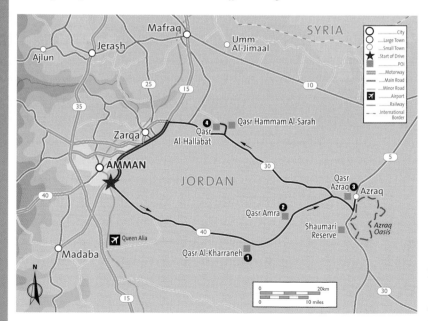

1 Qasr Al-Kharraneh

Located in an extremely desolate, barren landscape, this stark building is the most obviously defensive of the palaces (*see pp66–7*). Including a browse around the new Visitor Centre and refreshments tent, a visit takes about an hour.

Continue east along the road towards Azraq and Iraq, and after a further 15km (9 miles) a sign points left to Qasr Amra.

2 Qasr Amra

This tiny unassuming building is the biggest surprise of the palaces, because of its extraordinarily explicit frescoes depicting hedonistic lifestyles (*see pp58–9*). The new Visitor Centre shows how restoration work was completed. Allow a good hour again.

Continue another 26km (16 miles) along the main road to reach the trees that mark the edge of the Azraq oasis. Fork left at the junction to the north. To reach the fort at Azraq, continue a further 2km (1¼ miles) north on the main road until the black fort rises on your left at the edge of town. The Eco-lodge lies back some 600m (⅓ mile) south of the junction, if you want to break for lunch (see p167).

3 Qasr Azraq

Famous because of its more recent T E Lawrence associations, the fort was originally a Roman construction (*see pp62–3*). About half an hour should be all you will need to look around.

A bear playing a lute at Qasr Amra

Return to the main junction in south Azraq and follow the same road back towards Amman. After 9km (5½ miles) turn right towards Zarqa and follow this road for 44km (27 miles). Fork right at the sign for Qasr Al-Hallabat. This little road leads off for 3km (2 miles), passing the tiny Qasr Hammam Al-Sarah en route, to reach Qasr Al-Hallabat.

4 Qasr Al-Hallabat

Newly restored in 2007 and with a new Visitor Centre, this is one of the most extensive of the palaces, built over the remains of a Roman fortress, even boasting some floor mosaics (*see p63*).

Return to the main road and continue to Zarqa, following the signs to Amman, 40km (25 miles) further on.

The bleak façade of Qasr Al-Kharraneh

QASR AL-KHARRANEH

The most strikingly defensive of all the palaces, Qasr Al-Kharraneh is extremely well preserved, with two storeys and most rooms intact. Solid and square, the castle has interestingly decorated arrow-like slits, which were in fact ventilation slits for the inner rooms. The inscription over the gateway bears the date 711, though some believe it was originally a pre-Islamic building, possibly a Sassanid fort, since some of its architectural features, such as the tree of life medallion on its upper storey, show influences from Mesopotamia.

Its strategic importance is not immediately apparent to the layman, but in fact it lies at an important intersection of a number of tracks at the head of the wadi, and was used as a caravanserai by the traders from Syria to all points south and east. A well just outside the entrance supplied water to the castle and is still in use today. The new Visitor Centre is located a windswept and shadeless 400m (¹/₄-mile) walk away from the castle itself, which forces you to take in the bleakness of the surrounding landscape.

The long, vaulted downstairs rooms on either side of the entrance were camel stables. There were originally 99 rooms in the castle, the ground floor ones plain and simple and used as storerooms, the upper living quarters decorated with beautiful carved arches in the finely proportioned vaulted rooms. The most elaborately decorated room lies directly above the entrance gateway and was probably the caliph's own room. The outer walls are at least 1m (3¼ft) thick, built of local stone with earth and water mixed together to form a kind of bonding cement.

Two sets of steps lead to the carefully restored roof, offering fine views.

Refreshments are available in the Bedouin tent, and toilet facilities are to be found on-site.

Open: 8am–6pm (summer), 8am–4pm (winter). Admission charge covers Qasr Amra and Qasr Azraq as well (see pp58–9 & 62–3).

DRINKING WITH THE CALIPHS

All the Umayyad caliphs were fond of entertainment. Even Mu'awiya set aside the evenings for listening to tales of past heroes and historical anecdotes. The favourite drink, especially with the women, was rose sherbet, which is still drunk in Damascus and many Arab towns. Drinking was to become a progressive weakness in later caliphs. Abd Al-Malik, we are told, drank wine only once a month, though apparently when he did he drank so heavily that he would force himself to vomit afterwards to help him recover. Hisham drank once a week, after the Friday prayers, while Walid I drank every other day. Yazid drank daily, and trained a pet monkey to share in his revelry.

Walid II was definitely the most advanced, however, and there are eyewitness accounts of his drinking parties, in which he would have the bathing pool filled with wine, then swim in it, supposedly gulping enough to lower the level visibly. Accompanied by dancing and singing handmaidens, he would frolic in the liquid until they all lost consciousness. These Umayyad soirées, however, also produced much by way of music and above all poetry, some of which has survived.

Decorative elements on the exterior of Qasr Al-Kharraneh

QASR MUSHATTA AND QASR TUBA

These are the least visited of the remaining desert palaces, lying as they do off the standard desert palace circuit.

Qasr Mushatta

Still impressive, with high, vaulted brick domes almost like baths, and reused fine marble pillars from Roman sites, the ground plan of this palace is quite complex. Before 1903 it would have been even more impressive, since its entire façade was covered in elaborate and intricate carvings of vines, flowers, leaves and birds, but the Ottoman sultan of the time, Abdul Hamid, made a gift of the palace to the Kaiser, whereupon its sculptures were prised off and shipped to the Pergamon Museum in Berlin, where they can still be seen. A few fragments lying near the main palace entrance hint at what the whole façade might have looked like.

Thought to have been built in the 8th century by Walid II, it was never finished, since many labourers died from lack of water in the area, finally causing a revolt in which the caliph was killed. His successor Yazid III never made any attempt to complete this or any other of Walid's half-finished projects.

Now stranded on the northern perimeter of the airport, just beyond the fence, you have to reach this palace by circuiting the southern, then eastern, then northern perimeter, like three sides of a square. The checkpoint guards may ask you to show or leave your passport. It is unfenced and has no facilities at all.
Free admission.

Qasr Tuba

The most isolated of all the desert palaces, Qasr Tuba is large, but its brickwork is in poor repair. It was built in 744 but never finished.

WOMEN OF SUBSTANCE

The women of the early Umayyad days seem to have enjoyed what would now be regarded as an unusual degree of freedom. In Medina a proud and beautiful woman called Sukhaynah was noted not only for her beauty and learning, but also for her poetry, song and sense of humour. She once sent word to the chief of police that a Syrian had broken into her apartment. The chief himself rushed over to find her maid holding out a flea; Syria was ever noted for its fleas. Accounts of the numbers of her husbands range from seven to nine, and she frequently made complete freedom a precondition to the marriage.

Sukhaynah had a rival in the shape of Aishah, daughter of a Companion of the Prophet, living in Ta'if. She notched up only three husbands, but when the second chided her for not veiling her face, she retorted: 'Since Allah, may he remain blessed and exalted, hath put upon me the stamp of beauty, it is my wish that the public should view that beauty and thereby recognise his grace unto me. Under no conditions therefore will I veil myself.' She possessed the three qualities most prized in a woman among Arabs: noble descent, great beauty and a proud spirit.

A 4WD is required, together with a compass or guide to reach it, 50km (31 miles) south of Qasr Al-Kharraneh. The best approach is from the Amman–Aqaba desert highway, some 40km (25 miles) south of the airport, where a battered sign points off east into the desert. Like Qasr Mushatta, it is an unfenced site and offers no facilities. *Free admission.*

The remains of Qasr Mushatta

The King's Highway

The route that runs south from Amman to Petra along the ridge of mountains east of the Dead Sea has been known throughout history as 'The King's Highway'. It passes biblical sites, Crusader castles, Nabatean settlements and Roman cities, dropping down off the high plateau every now and again into spectacular valleys that are magnificent geological phenomena. The route offers a total contrast to the Desert Highway from Amman to Aqaba, which runs through endless wastelands of sand.

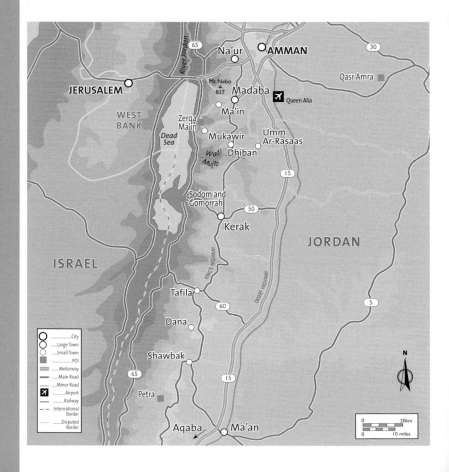

A rural scene on the King's Highway

The flat, straight Desert Highway route from Amman as far as Petra is 260km (162 miles) and can take as little as three hours. The King's Highway route, with its continuous variety of landscapes and relics from the past, is 274km (170 miles), and although it can be done in a day, that would only allow you time to stop off at the mosaics and churches of Madaba and at one of the Crusader castles. To do the route justice you should devote two days to it, stopping overnight at the pleasant hilltop resthouse of Kerak, just next door to the castle.

THE ROAD WELL TRAVELLED

The Bible tells how Moses, before leaving Egypt, sent messengers to the King of Edom (now southern Jordan) asking for permission to bring the people of Israel through his land: 'Let us pass, I pray thee, through thy country…We will go by the King's Highway, we will not turn to the right hand nor to the left, until we have passed thy borders.' (Numbers 20:17)

The Nabateans also used the route to transport cargoes of valuable spices from Persia to the Roman provinces in the west. The historic road did not fall from favour until the 16th century, when the Ottomans designated the desert highway the official pilgrim route to Mecca.

MADABA AND MOUNT NEBO

These two places offer Jordan's highest concentration of churches, reflecting the area's large Christian minority.

A good half-day should be allowed for a round trip from Amman to incorporate the Madaba mosaics and Mount Nebo.

Madaba

Madaba is known as the mosaic capital, for it was here that a school of mosaic craftsmen developed from the 4th century onwards, when Christianity gained a strong foothold. (The important Christian community here, some 40,000 of them, are mainly Greek Orthodox, but there is also a Melkite church and a Methodist mission.) Many of the mosaics were covered up by modern buildings, and until the museum recently appropriated it, one mosaic floor was in use as a garage.

Practicalities

The town is best reached by driving south from Amman towards the airport on the main desert highway, then forking off to the right where signposted. The total distance is 34km (21 miles).

St George Church

This is Madaba's chief treasure, the church with mosaic flooring (*see box*), that lies in the centre of town opposite the government resthouse. Though much of the mosaic is missing or damaged, it still gives a fascinating

MAP OF THE HOLY LAND

This is Jordan's most famous mosaic, on the floor of the functioning St George Church. The central point of the map is the city of Jerusalem, which is fortunately also one of the best-preserved sections. You can identify the Holy Sepulchre and the round dome of the Anastasius Church. Lower down is Bethlehem with its basilica, and on the right is the Jordan River, complete with fish – some emptying into the Dead Sea, others heading backwards, upriver, to escape the deadly water. The southern portion shows an area of the Nile Delta.

insight into the appearance of 6th-century towns.
Open: 7am–7pm (summer), 7am–6pm (winter). Closed: during services Fri 7–9am, Sun 7–10.30am. Admission charge.

Madaba Archaeological Park

This is Madaba's other high point, a collection of mosaics found in situ. A flight of steps leads up to the circular Church of the Virgin with a magnificent 7th-century geometric mosaic and a hall paved with a very fine mosaic depicting hunting and mythological scenes. By the ticket office, look out for the black and white mosaics which were found in the baths of Machaerus, Herod's Palace, which are the oldest in Jordan and date from the 1st century BC.
Open: Sat–Thur 8am–5pm, Fri 10am–4pm. Admission charge (includes Madaba Museum and the Church of the Apostles).

Mount Nebo

This is a superb vantage point, with views of the Jordan Valley and over the Dead Sea shimmering below to the west. On a clear day you can see the palms of Jericho and even Jerusalem. According to the Bible, this was the summit that God commanded Moses to climb in order to look over the Promised Land just before he died, and the atmosphere of the spot has a wonderful calm and serenity. Inside the Moses Memorial Church are extensive mosaics; especially impressive are the ones on the left.

Practicalities

From Madaba a sign points off to Mt Nebo, 10km (6 miles) away along a picturesque road leading to the church on the summit at 817m (2,680ft). No refreshments are available at the site, so bring all you need with you.
Open: 7am–7pm. Admission charge.

Mosaics at Moses Memorial Church in Mount Nebo

The Dead Sea

For most visitors to Jordan, a visit to the Dead Sea for a ritual float is a must. The drive from Amman takes you first through the town of Na'ur, where large numbers of Circassians were settled by the Ottoman Sultan Abdul Hamid. Once clear of Na'ur, the drive is a striking one, through barren lunar landscapes, as the road starts its descent into this, the deepest and most enclosed area on the earth's crust, 408m (1,339ft) below sea level and dropping.

Practicalities

This is an easy half-day excursion from Amman, as the total distance is only 50km (31 miles) and the drive takes about 45 minutes. It is signposted off the main road to the airport south from Amman, through Na'ur.

Naming the Dead Sea

Throughout its history the Dead Sea has been known by many names. The Hebrews called it the Sea of the Steppe, the Salt Sea or the Oriental Sea. The Greeks called it the Asphalt Lake from the pieces of black bitumen the lake was said to contain. The Nabateans sold the natural asphalt at high prices, notably to the Egyptians, who used it in the mummification of bodies. The Crusaders called it the Dead Sea, and the medieval Muslim geographers called it variously the

The shores of the Dead Sea are the lowest area of dry land on the planet

Stinking Lake, the Lake of Sodom and Gomorrah, and the Upside-down Lake.

Swimming

Serious swimming is impossible, as you cannot keep your limbs underwater to make the strokes, so to make any headway you have to make odd kicking and wriggling movements, propelling yourself along like some aquatic bug on the surface of the water. On the plus side, the low altitude here provides natural UV protection, reducing the need for sunblock. The salt content is ten times that of the Mediterranean, making the water feel oily and slimy on the skin. Fish carried down from the Jordan River die within a minute of arriving in the sea, and are found washed up on the shore, stiff and rigid with minerals.

Much of the Dead Sea shoreline is quite steep

DEATH OF THE DEAD SEA

Currently, the level of the lake drops by about 1m (3¼ ft) every year. Since the 1950s it has dropped by an alarming 25m (82ft). There are several reasons for this, the chief one being the increasing diversion of the freshwater sources away from the lake. The River Jordan is now just a trickle where it enters the Dead Sea, its waters and tributaries diverted by dams for irrigation projects. Another major factor is the potash and mineral industry which both Jordan and Israel have developed at the shallow southern end of the lake, an industry which relies on large-scale evaporation for its production. The surface area of the lake was over 1,000sq km (390sq miles) in the 1950s; now it is less than 700sq km (270sq miles).

At current rates of water loss the lake will dry up completely within 50 years, unless something drastic is done to solve the problem. Both the relevant Jordanian and Israeli authorities agreed in 2002 to implement the Red-Dead Canal, designed to bring seawater 250km (155 miles) north from Aqaba into the Dead Sea; the 400m (1,310ft) drop in altitude would mean that hydroelectric power could be generated along with shared desalination plants to ease the chronic water shortage in both countries. The project has been the victim of the political situation and has stalled indefinitely along with the Middle East peace talks.

In May 2009 the Jordanian government announced that it would implement a separate plan, the Jordan National Red Sea Development Project, to channel water from the Red Sea to the Dead Sea, with desalination plants along the way providing much-needed fresh water to Jordan. Environmentalists have expressed great concern about the chemical incompatibilities between the two seas and the impact of all the proposed schemes on local ecosystems.

ZERQA MA'IN

The excursion to the hot springs at Zerqa Ma'in is one of the most fun diversions off the King's Highway. The approach snakes down one of the steepest and most tortuous stretches of road in the country, through the cliffs with gradients sometimes reaching 15 per cent and dramatic views across to the Dead Sea.

A new road now continues from Zerqa Ma'in for the final 10km (6 miles) down the shoreline to join the Dead Sea highway that runs down the rift valley to reach the Red Sea at Aqaba. Turning left at the bottom you will soon come to the outlet of the Ma'in gorge at Ain Zara, identified with the ancient Callirhoe, where Herod the Great used to descend from his palace at nearby Mukawir to take the waters. The Dead Sea Spa Hotel is now located here.

Practicalities

The hot springs lie some 30km (19 miles) southwest of Madaba, and

The men's open-air pool at Zerqa Ma'in

the Ma'in Spa Hotel there makes an excellent and comfortable base for exploring the spectacular scenery of the area if you have a couple of days to spare. The hotel is very exclusive and families often stay for weeks at a time, taking the waters and walking in the gorge scenery below.

There are good toilet facilities and an expensive buffet restaurant for those on day trips.

Open: 6am–4pm. Admission charge for non-hotel guests to park in one of the car parks and have unlimited access to one of the three pool areas.

THERAPEUTIC TOURISM

Israel is way ahead of Jordan in the business of exploiting the beneficial properties of the Dead Sea and its springs. Jordanian skincare products from the Dead Sea are distributed only within the country, whereas the Israelis market theirs worldwide, and at higher prices. Both the waters and the mud have high concentrations of calcium, magnesium, bromine, sulphur and bitumen, a concoction which has been proven to improve dramatically many severe skin problems such as psoriasis, and joint problems like rheumatism. The specialist medical treatments on offer in the cluster of luxury Dead Sea hotels are often booked solid for months in advance.

Given the parlous state of the lake itself, it is highly debatable whether the continued growth of this industry is a good thing. All the fresh water used in the hotels and the irrigation of their landscaped gardens is piped in from Wadi Mujib. This is despite fierce protests from the Royal Society for the Conservation of Nature about the damage being done to the fragile ecosystems of the lower Wadi Mujib.

The main waterfall at Zerqa Ma'in

Taking the waters

The waters of Zerqa Ma'in vary in temperature between 55 and 60°C (130–140°F), though there are a few cold springs among the total of 60 or so. Surprising numbers of young Jordanian men come to take the waters here, which is why women tourists generally prefer to bathe in the enclosed separate women's area of the so-called Roman bath. Men can enjoy the open-air hot waterfalls that plunge spectacularly into the pool below. The facilities are clean and well maintained.

The site of Herod's Palace, overlooking the Dead Sea

HEROD'S PALACE AND UMM AR-RASAAS

These two sites are unusual and far less visited than most destinations on the King's Highway, but both make rewarding detours.

Herod's Palace (Mukawir)

Climb to the summit of the spectacular and atmospheric site of Herod's Palace. Here it was, the Bible tells, that Salome danced for the head of John the Baptist, and the eerie conical nest-like mound overlooking the Dead Sea seems a strangely fitting site. The distinctive, almost volcanic shape of the hill is unmistakable as you

JOHN THE BAPTIST'S HEAD

And the king was sorry: nevertheless for the oath's sake, and for them which sat with him at meat, he commanded it to be given her.

And he sent, and beheaded John in the prison.

And his head was brought in a charger, and given to the damsel; and she brought it to her mother. (Matthew 14:9–11)

approach. Little remains beyond foundations and walls, but the views are stunning and there is the fun of skipping about from room to room imagining where the dancing might have taken place. The graphic local name is Palace of the Gallows.

The causeway you climb to reach it was built as an access ramp by the Romans in AD 72 when they laid siege to the rebel Jews who had fled from Jerusalem to here – Jordan's version of the more famous Massada on the Israeli side of the Dead Sea. They then razed the palace to the ground, but enough remains to hint at the luxury it once enjoyed, with traces of lavish baths and mosaic flooring. Extensive storerooms for goods to withstand a siege lined the outer defensive walls, and three towers rose on the west, south and east sides.

Practicalities

Some 14km (8½ miles) after Madaba at Libb, a sign points right off the King's Highway to Mukawir, a little village

20km (12½ miles) away. The track beyond the village ends after a bumpy 2km (1¼ miles) in the car park opposite the ramp. The walk up the ramp to the summit takes about 15 to 20 minutes. This two-hour detour is recommended for those with the time and their own transport.
Open site. Free admission.

Umm Ar-Rasaas

Listed in 2004 as a UNESCO World Heritage Site, Umm Ar-Rasaas is a remote Byzantine settlement that boasts some splendid church mosaics in two of its fifteen churches, St Stephen (785) and Bishop Sergius (587), which are the largest and most complete in Jordan. The site is extensive, covering 2sq km (¾ sq mile), and has been under excavation since 1986.

The mosaics are protected under a locked roofed area. The one in St Stephen has illustrations from nature – seashells, animals, fruit and trees – with fishermen and the cities of the Nile Delta. Bishop Sergius' mosaic, meanwhile, shows Jerusalem and seven other cities, along with classical personifications of the Sea and the Earth.

Continuing 1.5km (1 mile) further beyond the site, look out to the right of the road for the impressive 15m (50ft)-high stone tower, thought to be that of a stylite hermit imitating St Simeon Stylites, living on top of his tower in seclusion with food and water pulled up by rope.
26km (16 miles) southeast of Madaba, 13km (8 miles) east of Dhiban. Open site. Free admission since guardian's hut is now abandoned.

The King's Highway

The Byzantine remains at Umm Ar-Rasaas

WADI MUJIB

Continuing south from Dhiban, you reach the edge of the spectacular Wadi Mujib after about 15km (9 miles). The 900m (2,950ft) descent into this Grand Canyon-like gorge is one of the most dramatic visual experiences that Jordan has to offer. An excellent road now hairpins down 9km (5½ miles) to the valley floor, with lush vegetation and cultivation even at the height of summer. The width of the gorge at the top is 4km (2½ miles) and the combined descent and ascent cover 20km (12½ miles) of snaking bends, with several spectacular viewing points towards the start of the descent. Whether it is the view that distracts so many drivers or the steepness that causes their brakes to fail, terrible accidents occur on this road with unfailing regularity, often involving lorries or buses, so drivers beware.

In the Old Testament the river which flows along the gorge was known as the Arnon, disgorging eventually into the Dead Sea. On the ascent, to the left of the road, two Roman pillars mark the passage of the original Roman road.

In 1998 a dam was built in the wadi, and the road across the wadi floor crosses the dam itself. The reservoir provides much-needed water supplies for the area, though its impact on the ecosystems both upstream and downstream has not been studied or assessed. Much of the surrounding territory now falls within the Wadi Mujib Nature Reserve.

Wadi Mujib Nature Reserve

Created in 1987 under the control of the Royal Society for the Conservation of Nature (RSCN) the reserve covers 212sq km (82sq miles) and has seven permanently flowing streams. It extends from the plateau at the King's Highway at an altitude of 900m (2,950ft) down to the Dead Sea shore at 400m (1,310ft) below sea level, making it the lowest nature reserve in the world. The biodiversity it incorporates, however, is surprising. The rare Syrian wolf is still found here, along with the Egyptian mongoose, foxes, caracals, striped hyenas, vipers and venomous desert cobras. A special enclosure has also been

The reservoir at Wadi Mujib

The dam at Wadi Mujib reservoir

established to breed the endangered Nubian ibex, a project which has so far met with considerable success.

Hiking in the Wadi Mujib

The wilderness hiking and canyoning on offer here are among the best in the entire Middle East. The Visitor Centre for the reserve is down by the Mujib Bridge where the river empties into the Dead Sea, and the reserve is open all year round. There are several hiking trails but admission to the reserve without permission is forbidden, so all trails and guides must be booked in advance with the RSCN. Numbers are also strictly controlled, with between 5 and 25 people walking with each guide.

The full-length trip of 36km (22 miles) from the King's Highway end to the Dead Sea takes two days and can only be completed from April to October because of the risk of flash floods. By starting at the village of Faqua (where there is an RSCN ranger post) you can condense the walk into a day. The final 1,500m (4,920ft) before the Dead Sea passes through the breathtaking Mujib Siq, an eerie narrow gorge with a 20m (66ft)-high waterfall and fine pools, is a fitting climax to a unique canyoning adventure. '

RSCN. Wild Jordan Centre, Amman. Tel: 06 533 7931. www.rscn.org.jo. Visitor Centre. 20km (12¹/₂ miles) south of the Dead Sea resort hotels. Tel: 03 231 3059. Admission charge.

Biblical scenery around the Dead Sea

SODOM AND GOMORRAH

But the men of Sodom were wicked and sinners before the Lord exceedingly.

Genesis 13:13

If you have time and are interested in seeing the sites of biblical history, you can make a short excursion (two-and-a-half hours) from Kerak down to the Dead Sea to view what is popularly believed to be the site of Sodom and Gomorrah, the evil 'Cities of the Plain'.

Here a flat, salty promontory called Al-Lisaan ('the tongue' in Arabic) juts out into the shallow basin of a relatively recent geological formation. The earthquake which caused it is popularly associated with the catastrophic event that destroyed Sodom and Gomorrah and resulted in Lot's wife being turned into a pillar of salt; certainly the character of the Dead Sea in these southern areas, with its salty, arid expanses, is quite different from the busy northern shore.

The cities destroyed

The Lord rained upon Sodom and Gomorrah brimstone and fire from the Lord out of heaven.

Genesis 19:24

The destruction of Sodom and Gomorrah was utter and no one survived to tell the tale. In fact, 2,500 years of silence followed the catastrophe, and the scene until the Byzantine era had been as desolate as the prophecies suggested. Dr Kyle (*see opposite*) puts it graphically: 'Here was a dead sea round about a dead land, and harbouring the memory of a moral character that was dead and a stench in the nostrils of the whole world.'

The cities discovered

The descent from Kerak is a striking one. At first the steep hillsides are covered in cultivation with terraces of olives, figs and vineyards all down the Wadi Kerak, then as you descend further the landscape changes to bare hills. The only visible remains here are at the site of Bab Al-Dhra'a, just to the right of the road, 2km (1¼ miles) after passing the village of Al-Dhra'a. Set some 190m (625ft) above the level of the Dead Sea, this is a vast Bronze Age settlement over 300m (985ft) long with a fortress, surrounded by massive rampart-like walls over 4m (13ft) thick in places.

This spot was discovered in the early 1920s by one Melvin Kyle, Doctor of Divinity in Jerusalem, who set out with a party of fellow theologians and archaeologists to find evidence for the existence of the cities of the plain. The dedicated team scoured the hillsides and shores of the southern Dead Sea and were rewarded with discoveries of the potsherds of a Canaanite civilisation of the 20th century BC, i.e. the early Bronze Age. From nearby graves and within the fortress of Bab Al-Dhra'a they collected several thousand flint artefacts, mainly knives. Their date, they concluded, coincided with the end of Sodom and Gomorrah, and there was no evidence to suggest subsequent occupation of the site.

These discoveries led them to deduce that Bab Al-Dhra'a was probably the Great High Place of Sodom and Gomorrah, where the inhabitants came on annual pilgrimages and performed pagan rites, 'the nature of which had better not be surmised', as Dr Kyle tactfully put it.

The site believed to be Sodom

KERAK CASTLE

The town of Kerak is totally dominated by its fortress, Jordan's finest Crusader castle, set on the hilltop summit at 950m (3,120ft). The name Kerak is a corruption of the Frankish Crusader name for Le Crac, which in turn is the same name as that given to the famous Crac des Chevaliers in Syria, the best-preserved Crusader castle in the world.

Practicalities

The approach road to the fort is well signposted as it winds up through the town to arrive directly in front of the fine resthouse. Entry is across a wooden footbridge spanning the moat to enter the castle precinct, where the ticket

Kerak Castle is built on a hilltop

office awaits you. No refreshments are available inside the complex, but outside the walls is an excellent restaurant with a terrace and good toilet facilities.

120km (75 miles) south of Amman.
Open: 8am–5pm. Admission charge.

The Crusaders

After the Abbasid Arabs moved their capital away from Damascus further east to Baghdad in 750, Jordan was distanced from the prosperity of the new empire and lay semi-forgotten and decaying. The arrival of the Crusaders brought the country into prominence again, for the region of Transjordan was the major principality of the Latin kingdom of Jerusalem, extending from Wadi Zerqa Ma'in in the north to the Gulf of Aqaba in the south, with Kerak as its capital. The fortress here, built in 1136, was the centre of all Crusader activity east of the Jordan, and other fortresses were built at Shawbak (called Monte Reale by the Crusaders), at Wadi Musa (Le Vaux Moyse) near Petra, and at Jezirat Far'oun (Isle de Graye), a small island in the Gulf of Aqaba.

The Crusader armies concentrated in these fortresses would attack the Muslim caravans and pilgrims that plied their way between Damascus, Mecca and Egypt, often in violation of truces. Kerak's most notorious lord, the French Raynald of Chatillon, was especially guilty of these violations, in return for which Saladin killed him with his own hand on capture.

The many layers of Kerak Castle

The fort is not the sole legacy of the Crusaders in this area; Kerak still has a significant minority of Christians, with both a modest Melkite and a Latin church.

The fortress

From afar the appearance of Kerak Castle is deceptive, for it seems to consist of nothing but defensive walls. In Crusader times the castle could be entered by three underground passages which led from the hillside under the walls directly into the enclosure. Two of the entrance tunnels can still be seen, one on the eastern hillside, the other to the northwest. The original Crusader gateway is blocked today.

The castle enclosure is large and extensive and you should allow a minimum of one-and-a-half hours to see it all properly. At first glance the whole place seems to be ruined, but as you walk further in, all the vaults and buildings below the current ground level come into view, with steps leading down in many directions to colossal vaulted tunnels and rooms, whose functions have been variously interpreted as banqueting halls, sleeping quarters and stables. A torch is handy in exploring the darker recesses. At the lower level is a museum built into one of the vaults, some 100m (330ft) long and 15m (50ft) wide.

The Crusades

Regard the Franj! Behold with what obstinacy they fight for their religion, while we, the Muslims, show no enthusiasm for waging holy war.

Saladin

The gulf of ignorance

European and Arab accounts of the Crusades have little in common. The Frankish Crusaders first set out to the Holy Land convinced that they were themselves far superior to the local Muslim population. They had no understanding of Islam and thought that Muslims were idolators worshipping Muhammad as a god. The incoming Franks were also hostile to the local Christian sects, especially the Greek Orthodox, and towards the resident Jewish communities. The Muslims, on the other hand, saw the Frankish Crusaders as infidels,

The heavily ruined Crusader Castle of Al-Woairah at Petra

SALADIN

Known in Arabic as 'Salah Ad-Din', Reformer of the Faith, the great Muslim warrior chief is considered to this day in the Arab world a paragon of virtue, with a keen sense of honour and justice. He fought only when absolutely necessary, was merciful towards his prisoners and accumulated no personal wealth. Far more than just a champion of Sunni Islam, Saladin also founded many religious schools and mosques, patronised scholars, encouraged theological studies and introduced advanced water systems with dykes and canals.

worshipping three gods in the form of God, Jesus and the Holy Ghost. Neither side realised the similarities between their faiths and the gulf of ignorance was huge.

For Arabs the 12th and 13th centuries were viewed as years spent repelling a brutal and destructive invasion of barbarian hordes. The Arabs did not speak of Crusades but of Frankish invasions, and 'franj' is the word used in colloquial Arabic even today to refer loosely to a Westerner. Contemporary accounts talk of the Crusaders' lack of refinement, their cruel treatment of Muslim prisoners, their frequent breaking of their truce promises, and even their poor hygiene. Washing and bathing are religious requirements for Muslims, whereas the Crusaders did not routinely wash and were distinctly smelly to Arab nostrils. The Crusaders' religious pretext for invading the region was never viewed by ruling Muslims as either credible or legitimate, since the indigenous Christians were not being persecuted, and Christians arriving peacefully on pilgrimage from Europe were allowed free passage to the Holy Land without interference.

The gulf bridged

At times of peace, however, which were after all much longer than times of war over the 200-year period spanned by the Crusades, there were many examples of good Muslim–Crusader relations. Safe conducts for travellers and traders were usually honoured, and local Muslim workmen and farmers were often employed by the Frankish knights to help build their castles and farm the surrounding land. Gradually the Franks began to adopt local habits, wearing looser clothing more suited to the climate, and enjoying the generous use of sugar and spice on their food. There was even occasional intermarriage with local women, and their mixed-blood offspring were called 'poulains', meaning 'young ones'.

The great divide that theoretically existed between the Muslim and Christian worlds was therefore sometimes more blurred than is presented these days by people who have been known to distort the facts to suit current popular thinking.

SHAWBAK CASTLE

Half an hour's drive north of Petra a sign points off to this dramatically sited Crusader castle. The little tarmac track, mercifully too narrow for coaches, leads 3km (2 miles) over the bare windblown hills to make a rear approach to the impressive castle, all alone on its conical hilltop. Deserted and dignified, its high walls make a good spot for a lofty picnic.

The site was chosen because it dominated the two main east–west routes to the Wadi Araba, and while the

Mameluke inscription at Shawbak Castle

surrounding landscape today looks bleak and desolate, the contemporary medieval descriptions reveal the valleys at that time to have been rich in corn, vineyards and olives. Fruits, especially apricots, were so abundant that many of them were exported to Egypt. In the 14th century around 600 people lived in and around the castle, mainly Christians, presumably the descendants of the original Frankish knights. As late as the 1960s, the castle was still inhabited by a number of peasant families who had built their dwellings and huts within the walls, but these people were persuaded to leave.

Practicalities

In the parking area the guardian sits with his friends, offering tea and a browse through his fine collection of rocks and bric-a-brac. He will guide you around if you like, and since there is no formal entry fee, a tip of JD1–2 is appreciated.

The fortress

Though badly ruined, a fair amount still remains to be seen. The original structure, called Monte Reale, was built in 1115 by Baldwin I as part of a chain of fortresses to protect the route from Damascus to Egypt. It was captured in 1189 by Saladin after a year and a half of siege. After Saladin's conquest the castle remained in Ayyubid hands for nearly 70 years, and the inscriptions built into the main entrance gateway date from this period. After 1260 the

Shawbak Castle sits on its own mound

Mamelukes chose Shawbak as their headquarters for controlling southern Jordan, rebuilding and restyling much of the castle. In the 19th century the Ottomans under Ibrahim Pasha made further changes when they used the place as a barracks.

These differences of period and reconstruction are evident in the different types and colour of building blocks. As at Kerak, the Franks used large blocks of the hard, black volcanic rock found locally, while the Muslims built from softer greyish or yellowish limestone, more carefully dressed and in wider blocks, brought from a more distant quarry. Inside the walls above the entrance gateway are the remains of two churches, and crosses can still be seen carved into the walls.

THE WATER OF LIFE

Higher up on the hill is an entrance shaft leading down 375 slippery stone-cut steps into the depths of the hillside to a well. With a powerful torch and shoes with a good grip, it is still possible to make the descent right down to water level. This remarkably labour-intensive construction, thought to be unique in Crusader architecture, gave Monte Reale the safe water supply it needed to hold out against Saladin considerably longer than its sister castle Kerak, to the north.

Petra

Without doubt a visit to Petra will be the high point of any visit to Jordan. Chosen in 2007 as one of the New Seven Wonders of the World, Petra ranks alongside the Pyramids of Giza, the Taj Mahal and Machu Picchu as one of the world's great sites.

Inevitably, a site of such stature attracts a lot of development, and unfortunately the former village of Wadi Musa that guards the entrance to Petra is now an ugly, sprawling town of hotels, shops and attendant businesses, all living off the tourist trade. Even this, however, cannot detract from the amazing phenomenon that is the ancient site of Petra.

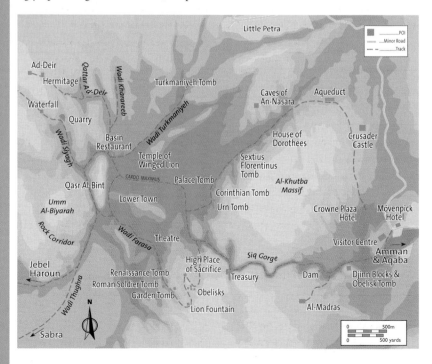

Detail on the façade of the Treasury

A natural phenomenon

Even as you begin to drop into the valley of Wadi Musa you will notice the change in landscape. Gradually the rocks and hillsides all around take on strange and distinctive formations, often showing hints of red, mauve, yellow, blue and black. The rock city of Petra sits in the middle of this huge geological freak of nature, over 200sq km (80sq miles) in area. Earthquakes, watercourses, wind and rain have carved out of the soft natural sandstone a fantasy landscape where dramatic, puffy rock formations suddenly give way to abrupt gorges, narrow defiles and deep fissures.

A man-made phenomenon

In some ways even more remarkable than the natural phenomenon is the man-made contribution here, for the Nabatean architects of Petra were no more than a humble tribe of nomad camel-drivers from the deserts of northern Arabia. It has been suggested that Petra may have been one of the first permanent settlements used by nomads, around the 4th century BC.

From their capital at Petra they established an elaborate network of caravan routes which brought spices, incense, myrrh, gold, silver and precious stones from India and Arabia, to be traded on to the West. From the wealth they acquired they adorned their city with palaces, temples, arches and monumental ways. Most of those that were free-standing have largely disappeared, but many were carved into the rock – the Treasury, the monumental tombs, the High Place of Sacrifice – and these still remain today in a condition of perfection so staggering that you feel you have entered a time warp.

When to go

Seasons

The site is open officially from 7am to 6pm but in practice from dawn to dusk. The best months for a visit are March to May and September to November. From December to February it can be very cold, especially at night, with frequent snow showers, since the altitude of the central Petra basin is surprisingly high at 1,000m (3,280ft). From June to August it is extremely hot, although you have the advantage of longer evenings, which means that you can rest from noon until 2pm during the heat of the day.

Tourists

At busy periods like Fridays and holidays, Petra can get up to 3,000 visitors in a single day. On a normal day it is around 1,500, and anything less than 1,000 is considered a quiet day. So it's best to avoid Fridays and holidays if you don't want the crowds to detract from the experience. That said, the site is so huge, there are always places you can go to escape the crowds (*see pp122–5*).

How long to stay

The town of Wadi Musa that serves Petra offers no more than 1,200 beds, so many visitors come just on day trips from Aqaba or Amman. For a proper visit you should aim to spend at least two nights here, or better still, three, so that you can enjoy a full couple of days exploring the extensive site.

How to get there

At 260km (162 miles) from Amman, the drive to Petra generally takes around three-and-a-half hours on the Desert Highway and six hours via the King's Highway. Day trips by JETT bus leave daily at 6am (6.30am in winter) and return at 3.30pm (3pm in winter). The ticket includes a meal in Petra but not the increasingly steep admission charge.

Admission charge

Be warned that prices have become astronomical in recent years. There are separate rates for Jordanians and other Arabs, as opposed to foreigners, whose ticket includes a horse ride through the Siq and back, plus brochures. One-day, two-day and three-day passes are all available, and children under 15 go free, however there is no student discount. Cards are not accepted; only cash in JD.

The stepped pyramid motif is common in this region

The rock-cut theatre at Petra

Preparing for your visit

First and foremost, you will need to be in a reasonable state of fitness to fully appreciate what the site has to offer, since the amount of walking is considerable, often uphill along gruelling paths and on uneven surfaces. Almost as important is your footwear. Make sure you are wearing comfortable shoes or boots that will cope with the loose and often rocky ground. Next most important is protection from the sun; you need loose clothing, and a hat or sun cream – preferably both. You will also need water; carry a small bottle on you to make sure you do not get dehydrated. A small snack of the non-melting kind, such as nuts or a cereal bar, is also a good idea.

Facilities

These days there is no shortage of places to buy soft drinks within the site and there are now several proper restaurants all grouped in the Qasr Al-Bint area, an hour's walk in from the entrance. Prices are high though, and you may prefer to bring a simple picnic that does not weigh too much. Toilet facilities are very limited, really just within the proper restaurants, and the great outdoors generally has to suffice.

Photography

Make sure you remember your camera, since Petra is one of the world's most photogenic places. Timing is important though, to get the sun falling correctly. The sun strikes the façade of the Treasury at 9–10am in winter, 8.30–9.30am in summer. Regarding the other great monumental façade, Ad-Deir, the sun does not strike until the afternoon, from 2pm onwards. Two walks, one short, one long, are given in this chapter and these incorporate the timings to best advantage.

Short walk: Petra

This walk around the main sites of Petra takes a full day but at a leisurely pace, so that you can enjoy frequent rest stops along the way. If the level of physical exertion is more than you are happy with, you can always take the free horse ride or pay for a carriage as far as the Treasury, then ride a donkey up to Ad-Deir. There is no shortage of young boys offering these services en route.

The total distance covered is about 6km (4 miles). For the best timing, set off at around 8.30am. The return journey from the furthest point,

Ad-Deir, with plenty of stops, will take about two or three hours, so you should arrive back at the entrance no later than 6pm.

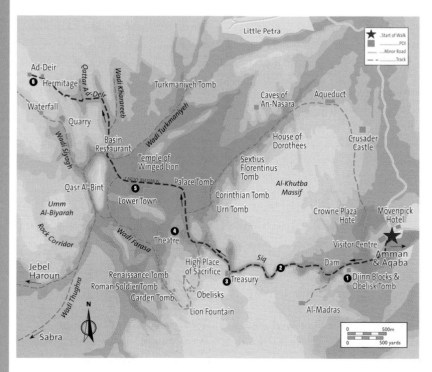

Descend from wherever your hotel is to the Visitor Centre, beside which is the ticket office where you must buy your pass. Your ticket must then be shown again at the gateway entrance to Petra proper.

1 Djinn Blocks and Obelisk Tomb

After a gentle ten-minute stroll slightly downhill, you will come to three gigantic blocks of stone on your left, which served as strange, hollow, multi-storey tombs (*see p96*). A little further on your left, carved into the rock face, is the unmistakeable Obelisk Tomb (*see p97*), your first taste of what is in store once inside the city.

Walk on for another few minutes along the path to reach the entrance of the Siq, the narrow gorge which is the entry approach to the city. Notice the remains of the dam to the right.

2 The Siq

This spectacular narrow gorge should not be rushed. Take a good half hour, examining the traces of the water channels and the rock colours along the way (*see p97*).

Emerge opposite the Treasury.

3 The Treasury

This is Petra's most famous site, the magnificent Treasury façade (*see p100*). Arrive between 8.30 and 10am to get the perfect lighting for photos.

Follow the wide main path as it winds on a little way further to reach the Theatre on your left.

4 The Theatre

Cut from the rock, the colours are wonderful, and the acoustics are still excellent – as many tour groups will demonstrate (*see p104*).

Continue on the main path to where it ends at the Lower Town and a cluster of restaurants.

5 The Lower Town

Here is a range of interesting buildings to explore, notably Qasr Al-Bint (*see pp104–5*). When you have seen as much as you want, have a leisurely lunch in one of the restaurants here.

From the bridge over the wadi by the Basin Restaurant, a small rocky path to the right begins the winding ascent to Ad-Deir, where the afternoon sun will be striking its façade.

6 Ad-Deir

This monastery is Petra's second most famous site (*see p105*).

Retrace your steps to the Lower Town and on up past the Theatre and Treasury, to re-enter the Siq and return to the entrance gate.

The decoration on top of the Treasury

From the site entrance through the Siq

The sites of Petra are described here and on pages 100–101 and 104–5 in the order in which you come to them on a standard visit.

Bab As-Siq (Gateway to the Siq)

As you set off from the entrance gate, the valley is, at this stage and for the first 15 to 20 minutes of your trip, quite wide and open. The first monuments you pass in this section are the curious **Djinn Blocks** ('Djinn' is Arabic for spirit or ghost, from which our word

PETRA'S GRAVES

Some 107 grave chambers with benches have been found throughout Petra, and it is thought that some of them were probably used purely for domestic purposes, like eating or even sleeping, rather than having specific funerary associations.

'genie' is derived), a cluster of three freestanding rock cubes just to the right of the track. All three are thought to have been grave chambers. The largest has a deeply grooved exterior which bears the crow-step pattern, a common Nabatean decoration and

The Obelisk Tomb on the approach to the Siq

hallmark of Petra thought to have its origins in Babylon.

Continuing along the main path you come to the **Obelisk Tomb** carved out of the cliff on the left. It dates from the 1st century AD, the period of the last Nabatean kings, and shows a strange mix of influences – Egyptian in the pyramid-like obelisks, and classical in the pillars, pediments and statue niche. It is in fact two superimposed tombs: the upper one with four obelisks and the lower one a triclinium, a grave chamber with rock benches round three sides.

The Siq

Just after the right-hand bend in the valley you reach the entrance to the Siq gorge itself, by walking up a small ramp over a dam, then dropping back down again to the level of the gorge. This dam was built to seal off the Siq entrance after a group of 23 tourists was drowned in a flash flood in 1963.

In Nabatean times the entire length of the Siq was paved with limestone blocks, only fragments of which remain today. At its narrowest point the gorge is a bare 2m (6½ft) wide, which makes the 100m (330ft)-high cliffs seem even more dramatic. The colours of the rock are mainly reds and browns, eroded into strange shapes by aeons of wind and water. Fragments of rock stairways can be seen at many points, leading off tantalisingly to neglected sanctuaries hidden in the cliffs.

The beautiful colours of the rock in the Siq

WATER SYSTEMS

While constructing the new Siq dam, the modern builders came across traces of an original Nabatean dam and water channels, and were able to build on the old foundations to some extent. Evidently the Nabateans, too, had wanted to use the Siq as the entrance to the city all year round, so had to protect it from winter floods. They had also devised an elaborate water system for their needs, whereby water was channelled along canals cut into the rock wall of the Siq. These channels can still be seen, especially on the left-hand side of the gorge, running at about head height. On the right-hand side are some sections of ceramic water pipe.

The Nabateans

A nomadic tribe from northern Arabia, the Nabateans began to move northwards into the biblical land of Edom in the early 6th century BC, gradually displacing the indigenous Edomite population. They emerged as a powerful and independent force by the 4th century BC, with their base at Petra. Its attractions were evident: a naturally defensive position, safe water supplies, fertile farming and grazing land, all combined with a strategic location near the junction of the silk and spice trade and caravan routes to the north and east. The name 'Nabatean' comes from the Arabic root 'nabat', meaning 'core' or 'innermost heart'.

The Nabateans' elaborate water system in the Siq

Nabatean gods

They brought with them from the Arabian Peninsula their worship of idols, their main gods being the male Dushara and the female Al-Uzza. She was a fertility goddess identified with caravans and the morning star, while he, literally 'He of Sharra', was named after the Sharra mountains of the Petra region. These mountains are called 'Seir' in the Old Testament, and Jehovah is also called 'He of Seir', suggesting that they were one and the same god. The Greeks later assimilated Dushara with Dionysus. Both Dushara and Al-Uzza are generally represented throughout Petra as blocks of stone or obelisks.

Nabatean temperament

In character the Nabateans were known to have been unwarlike and hard-working. From the accounts written by Strabo, the classical historian of the 1st century BC, a picture comes across of a peace-loving, industrious people whose cities were not walled. When they were threatened with attack, their preferred tactic, rather than fighting, was to buy off their enemies with valuable gifts. They managed this successfully

Parts of the Nabateans' original paving can still be seen in the Siq

with the Greeks and Romans, and during the turbulent history of the region they managed to remain in practice largely independent. When the last Nabatean king died in AD 106, Petra was incorporated into the new Roman province of Arabia, and became its capital.

The Romans and after

The Romans moved in and redesigned the city, building the main colonnaded street, the temples and baths. From the 2nd century onwards, the Roman caravan city of Palmyra in Syria took much of Petra's wealth as the trade routes changed and moved further north. As in the remainder of the region, Christianity made an early impact on the population, and by the 4th century Petra had its own bishop and one of the Nabatean tombs was converted into a church.

The population dwindled over the next few centuries and nothing more is heard of Petra until the 12th century, when the Crusaders settled there briefly, building two castles, one inside and the other just outside the main valley. From then until the 19th century the city sank into oblivion, thought of by learned Europeans as a fabled city of legendary wealth, like Atlantis. It was rediscovered in 1812 by the young Anglo-Swiss explorer James Burckhardt (*see p21*), who entered disguised as a Muslim with a guide on the pretext of making a sacrifice to Aaron. So it was that Burckhardt's were the first European eyes in six centuries to behold the Treasury façade.

From the Treasury to the High Place of Sacrifice

The Treasury (Al-Khazneh)

The walk through the Siq takes little more than half an hour yet it somehow seems longer because of all the twists and turns and because only rarely can you see more than 20m (65ft) ahead of you. All the more remarkable, then, is the moment when you first see, appearing in an unreal vision of sudden light, the magnificent façade of the Treasury awaiting you at the end of the blackened gorge.

The Bedouin call the Treasury 'Al-Jerrah' (the Urn) after the 4m (13ft)-high urn that sits on top of the upper storey. Local superstition holds that in this urn is hidden Pharaoh's treasure. The urn itself is consequently the most damaged section of the façade, pockmarked with the rifle shot of relentless attempts to dislodge it or break it open to release the treasure. In fact, like the remainder of the monument, it is solid rock. The Treasury's sheltered position has helped preserve the façade's other architectural outlines and decorative friezes and statues.

Its original purpose and even the exact date of its construction have long remained a mystery. Some scholars dated it to the 1st century BC, others to the 1st or 2nd centuries AD, but recent research has dated it to Aretas IV, who died in AD 40. Some thought it was a temple to Isis/Tyche, the goddess represented in the centre of the upper storey holding a cornucopia, while others thought it must be the monumental tomb of a king.

The High Place of Sacrifice

Some 200m (650ft) after the Treasury, a sign points left up to this special place. The steep climb up rock steps and corridors takes about 35 minutes and is impressive for its sense of ascending into a different world, hushed and remote from the heart of Petra. It has the feel of a ceremonial way, and priests would indeed have led processions up to make their ritual sacrifices at this, the most important of Petra's many high places. The two 7m (23ft)-high obelisks marked the entrance to the sanctuary, beside a heavily ruined fort. The cult installations are to be found a little higher up on the summit, carved into the natural sandstone, with an altar, steps and channels to collect the blood from the sacrificed animals. Nothing is

A UNIQUE MIX

Most scholars feel that foreign workmen and architects must have been brought in to work on the Treasury, since so many elements are alien to Nabatean design. The columns and capitals are Corinthian in inspiration, the giant obelisks are Egyptian, and the Tyche/Isis statue shows marked Alexandrian influence (Petra had extensive trading links with Alexandria). Scattered about in the various architectural features are winged sphinxes, a lion, a panther, a snake and dancing Amazons. The interior, in stark contrast, is almost totally plain.

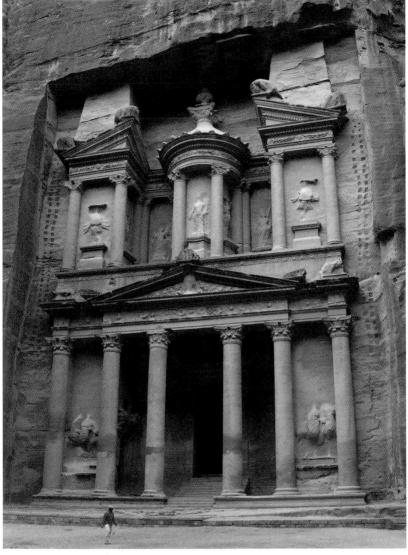

The magnificent façade of the Treasury

known for certain about the nature of the ceremonies which took place here, but the views from this summit are stunning, and you can even see the tiny white shrine of the Prophet Aaron on top of Jebel Haroun, revered by Muslims and a place of pilgrimage for the devoted.

Long walk: Petra

This walk represents about the maximum it is possible to do in a day, especially if you choose to walk rather than ride the full length of the Siq. It makes an excellent introduction to Petra, involving two longish climbs, one in the morning, the other in the afternoon. The itinerary assumes the pace of someone with a good level of fitness, and allows for fewer rests than the short walk (see pp94–5).

The total distance is about 9km (5¹/₂ miles). Ideally, you should set off no later than 8am and return around 6pm.

Follow the path from the site entrance for 700m (¹/₂ mile) until you see the little path to the left, after the Obelisk Tomb but before the Dam, that leads 400m (¹/₄ mile) up to Al-Madras.

1 Al-Madras

This attractive detour is up a series of rock-cut steps, leading to a cult sanctuary area (*see pp122–3*).
Return to the main path and continue to the Siq entrance.

2 The Siq

It takes about 25 minutes to walk slowly through the Siq, examining everything en route, and enjoying the unique feel of the gorge as it narrows (*see p97*).
The Siq ends directly opposite the Treasury.

3 The Treasury

This magnificent façade of the Treasury is Petra's most famous monument, and you should linger, aiming to arrive between 8.30 and 10am for the best lighting. Look out for the pockmarked urn on the upper storey (*see p100*).
Just 200m (650ft) beyond the Treasury, look out for the sign to the left that points up to the High Place of Sacrifice, leading up some worn rock-cut steps.

4 The High Place of Sacrifice

The ceremonial ascent takes about 35 minutes to arrive at the two obelisks. Above them is the altar and sacrificial area cut into the rock (*see pp100–101*).
Return to the obelisks and continue on the small path straight on, instead of turning left to drop back down to the theatre area. This path leads down steep stone steps and along a narrow stone corridor past a lion fountain, to descend into the Wadi Farasa.

5 Wadi Farasa

At the foot of the staircase you will see the Garden Tomb, a fine classical façade with a staircase on the right leading up to a huge cistern. Lower down, a series of other tombs is cut into the cliff face.

From here it is a shadeless 30-minute walk to the north to reach the Lower Town and its most interesting building, Qasr Al-Bint (see pp104–5).

6 Lower Town

Have a well-earned lunch in one of the restaurants, and enjoy your surroundings.

From the bridge over the wadi beside the Basin Restaurant, follow the small rocky path to the left that winds up to reach Petra's second most important monument. The walk should take approximately one hour.

7 Ad-Deir

This superb façade is west-facing and therefore enjoys afternoon sunshine (*see p105*). Those who have still not had enough of climbing can clamber right up on to the central urn from the rocks on the left side of the façade.

Return by the same path to the Lower Town and head up the Cardo Maximus, looking at the other monumental tomb façades en route, finally reaching the Treasury. Walk or ride back up through the Siq to the site entrance.

Little Petra

★ ...Start of Walk
■ ....POI
— ....Minor Road
— — ....Track

Ad-Deir
❼ Hermitage
Waterfall
Quarry
Basin Restaurant
Qasr Al-Bint ❻
Umm Al-Biyarah
Rock Corridor
Jebel Haroun
Sabra

Qattar
Ad-Deir
Wadi Kharareeb
Turkmaniyeh Tomb
Wadi Turkmaniyeh
Wadi Siyagh
Temple of Winged Lion
CARDO MAXIMUS
Lower Town
Wadi Farasa
Theatre
Renaissance Tomb
Roman Soldier Tomb
Garden Tomb
Wadi Thughra

Caves of An-Nasara
Aqueduct
House of Dorothees
Crusader Castle
Sextius Florentinus Tomb
Palace Tomb
Al-Khutba Massif
Corinthian Tomb
Urn Tomb
Crowne Plaza Hotel
Mövenpick Hotel
Visitor Centre
Amman & Aqaba
❹ High Place of Sacrifice
❸ Treasury
Obelisks
Lion Fountain
❷
Siq
Dam
Djinn Blocks & Obelisk Tomb
❶ Al-Madras

N

0   500m
0   500 yards

From the Theatre to Ad-Deir
The Theatre

Some 300m (330yds) beyond the Siq you come to the Theatre on your left. Despite heavy weathering it is still impressive for its size and for the work it must have entailed to cut 40 rows of seats out of the rock. Dating, like the Treasury, to the time of Aretas IV in the 1st century AD, it was later reworked by the Romans after they took Petra in 106, but all the masonry collapsed in the violent earthquake of 363. It would have held some 8,000 spectators.

Qasr Al-Bint (Palace of the Maiden)

Dominating the Lower Town, this is the most important Nabatean temple at Petra and was built in the 1st century BC. The maiden referred to is thought to have been the Pharaoh's daughter, who lived in the temple but deplored the lack of water. She announced she would marry the man who laid on a water supply to the palace, and someone must have succeeded, as excavations have revealed a stone water channel and drain at the foot of the temple.

The imposing façade is made from blocks of local sandstone and still rises

Qasr Al-Bint dominates the Lower Town

in places to about 25m (82ft) high. At the heart of the temple is the holy of holies where the sacred object, the statue of a deity, would have stood on the raised central platform. The human busts which once adorned the niches were destroyed in a fit of iconoclasm. The temple fell into disuse in the late Roman period, but was reused in Byzantine and medieval times when it seems to have been adapted to serve as living quarters or stables.

Ad-Deir (The Monastery)

The climb to Ad-Deir is for many the most exciting and memorable excursion at Petra. Exceptionally scenic with magnificent vistas throughout, it is a round trip of about two-and-a-half hours from the Qasr Al-Bint area, and passes on the ascent the Lion Triclinium tomb, a rock sanctuary (Qattar Ad-Deir) and an early Christian hermitage.

Five minutes beyond this you find yourself quite suddenly on the edge of a huge open sandy terrace with the colossal rock façade of Ad-Deir dwarfing you to the right. At 45m (148ft) high and 50m (165ft) wide, it is easily the largest monument in all Petra. Even the urn on top is 10m (33ft) high. Its name, the Monastery, originates from the number of small crosses carved into the interior rear wall, which suggest that the place was used by the early Christians of Petra in the 4th century, attracted by its isolated position.

The start of the route up to Ad-Deir

It is thought to have originally been a Nabatean temple, but some experts also consider it may have been the unfinished tomb of one of the Nabatean kings, unfinished because the niches appear never to have held any statues or decoration. Like the Treasury it is dated to the 1st century, and the two bear a strong resemblance, though the Monastery's stone colour is much yellower and its lines much bolder and more imposing. Lovers of heights will not be able to resist clambering up to the urn via the worn steps to the left of the façade.

Wadi Rum

An hour's drive from Petra or Aqaba, and four hours' drive from Amman on the Desert Highway, Wadi Rum is a world apart. Jordan's highest mountain, Jebel Rum, stands here at 1,754m (5,755ft), in the centre of an area of stunning desert landscapes. Despite its beauty, it is an exceptionally harsh environment in which to survive, and only the country's hardiest Bedouin are able to live here, thanks to their camels, their intimate knowledge of the water sources, and their perfectly adapted nomadic lifestyle.

Today Wadi Rum is a highly regulated visitor attraction, with the entire local population supported by the tourism industry. This has its pros and cons. With stricter regulation, there has inevitably been a loss in the complete experience of wilderness that used to accompany an independent traveller's camping trip to Wadi Rum. But on the other hand, the facilities now on offer, with comfortable tents, toilets and set rates for local guides, have meant that the wadi has become safely accessible to a much wider range and number of people, who might otherwise not have ventured into such terrain.

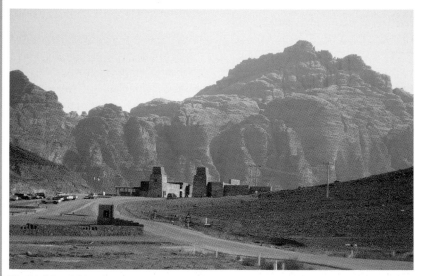

The Wadi Rum Visitor Centre

Certain areas are accessible only by 4WD

The area of Wadi Rum will forever be associated with the British Army Officer T E Lawrence, aka Lawrence of Arabia (*see pp12–13*), whose hauntingly memorable description of the landscape is as follows:

We looked up on the left to a long wall of rock, sheering in like a thousand-foot wave towards the middle of the valley… The crags were capped in nests of domes, less hotly red than the body of the hill… They gave the finishing semblance of Byzantine architecture to this irresistible place:

this processional way greater than imagination… Landscapes, in childhood's dream, were so vast and silent.

T E Lawrence,
Seven Pillars of Wisdom, 1922

To get anywhere near the level of expectation which Lawrence's account arouses, you must spend a sunset, a night and at least one full day in Wadi Rum. A day trip from Aqaba or Petra will only give you the merest flavour, so aim to incorporate at least one night here into your itinerary.

Time spent in Wadi Rum is always magical, especially at sunrise or sunset. There is a surprising amount of butterfly and bird life in the valley, and as you lie back in the sand gazing up at the towering rocks and the sky, the only sound is the birds soaring above and the gentle gusts of wind in your hair. At sunset the open valleys and weird rock shapes take on a surreal glow. By moonlight, too, the mountains give off an eerie glimmer.

Practicalities

A full range of tours is available by both 4WD and camel once you have paid your admission charge for the Wadi Rum protected zone beyond the Visitor

The Seven Pillars of Wisdom, seen from the Wadi Rum Visitor Centre

Centre. Obviously with a 4WD you can go much further, reaching such places as the Burdah Rock Bridge in an hour instead of requiring an overnight expedition by camel. The 4WD routes are now strictly controlled to minimise damage to the fragile ecosystems, and a team of conservation managers has been employed to patrol the 720sq km (278sq mile) protected area. Hunting and littering are two of the most common problems. In your own 4WD it is essential to stick to the designated tracks, and climbing and camping are now permitted only in the official campsites.

Visitor Centre. Tel: 03 209 0600. www. wadirum.jo. Email: rum@nets.com.jo. For short tours (i.e. less than a day) you can just turn up and take the next guide on the roster. For longer trips, email at least a week in advance, longer if booking in April, September or October.

Burdah Rock Bridge

Probably the most exhilarating and exciting excursion in Wadi Rum is the climb up to the natural rock bridge known as Burdah. With the help of a guide you can climb to the bridge in about an hour, slightly less on the descent. Although generally straightforward, the climb has its tricky moments, and is best avoided at midday in August; the rock can get extremely hot underfoot. Wear suitable clothing, since descending rock chimneys in a skirt or dress, for example, is not especially good for checking where you're putting your feet.

Khazali Canyon

This is a narrow gorge in the mountains, about 5km (3 miles) from Rum village, with many rock inscriptions.

Lawrence's Spring

Approximately 1km (²/₃ mile) south of Rum village is the spot where Lawrence is reputed to have washed during the Arab Revolt. Nearby are some interesting rock inscriptions.

Seven Pillars of Wisdom

This is the name given to the mountain that guards the entrance to the Wadi Rum corridor, with its seven distinctive pillar shapes. As you arrive at the Visitor Centre it is immediately to the left.

BEDOUIN SHIPS OF THE DESERT

In Wadi Rum and the other desert areas of Jordan there are still eight main nomadic tribes, some 40,000 people in all, having dwindled from around 220,000 in the 1950s. Many are now semi-nomadic, with a fixed base where most of the tribe stays, while only a small group, usually the young men, go off into the desert with the camels in search of grazing. Life in the desert without a camel is inconceivable and enormous care is taken of them. Arabian camels can live to the age of about 50. They mate for life when they are two and camel calves are generally born each year in autumn.

Glubb Pasha

The remarkable Englishman Sir John Bagot Glubb lived for 36 years among the Arabs. The first 19 years were almost entirely with them, and during this time he only rarely met Europeans and did not speak English for weeks on end. He made a conscious decision to resign his commission in the British Army to be with the Arabs, admitting that it was an emotional decision: 'I loved them' (*A Soldier with the Arabs*, 1957).

Founder of the Camel Corps
Glubb became an officer in the Arab Legion in 1930 and the following year formed the Desert Patrol based in Wadi Rum, affectionately known as the Camel Corps. Their role was to control dissident tribes and to patrol Jordan's borders. Today their job is merely to check on tribal movements, to rescue sheep from starvation by transporting them to waterholes, and generally to monitor any grievances. The force still numbers some 1,000 men, but the specially trained camels have dwindled from 150 to a mere 40.

Commander of the Arab Legion
In 1939 Glubb was asked by King Abdullah to assume command of the Arab Legion, the army of the little state of Transjordan, after which he was obliged to live in the capital and meet with royalty, presidents, ministers and ambassadors. He wrote poignantly in his book that 'from 1932 to 1948 the whole of Jordan

The Camel Corps is based in Wadi Rum

was one of the happiest little countries in the world'. He honestly believed that the differences between the Arab and Western outlook and temperament could complement one another.

From 1921 to 1951 there had been a genuine friendship and confidence between Jordan and Britain. But after the state of Israel was created on its border in 1948, and King Abdullah was assassinated in 1951, it all went wrong. Jordan absorbed the West Bank, introducing a new population and tensions with the existing Jordanians.

Glubb had led the Arab Legion across the Jordan to occupy the West Bank, not expecting to have to fight for it. He had begun during his time in the capital to gain insights into the workings of international affairs, and felt the West had become too dominant over Asia, not intentionally, but because their industrial progress had produced great wealth.

Members of the Desert Patrol

An English ending

In 1956 he was dismissed as commander of the Arab Legion by King Hussein. Hussein had always been a close personal friend of Glubb, but the king wanted to distance himself from the British and needed to demonstrate to his Arab critics that Glubb was not the real ruler of Jordan. He and Glubb had differed over defence arrangements, the promotion of Arab officers and the funding of the Arab Legion. Glubb returned to England and spent the rest of his life writing books about the Middle East and his experiences in the Arab world. 'I failed hopelessly,' he wrote, 'in the task to which I devoted nearly all my life…'

Glubb died in Sussex in 1986. He had married in 1938 and had a son, Godfrey, born in Jerusalem and named after the Crusader king. Glubb subsequently adopted a Bedouin girl and two Palestinian refugees, a boy and girl. Godfrey converted to Islam as a young man and became a prominent journalist writing about the Palestinian cause.

Camel ride: Wadi Rum

Camels are the most ecologically sound way to travel in the desert, and of course the most traditional. A full range of tours is on offer, from a 30-minute taster to the full overnight trekking experience, but whatever you choose, the experience will stay with you far longer than the inevitable stiffness that ensues from using muscles that you didn't even know existed.

Camel treks are no longer the major organisational feat they were just a decade or so ago. Now, with the Visitor Centre (*see pp108–9*) controlling prices and organising set routes according to fixed timings and levels of difficulty, the whole business is far more straightforward and not nearly as daunting as it used to be.

This trek to the Alameleh inscriptions is the best of the short camel rides on offer, and starts, like all of them, at Rum village.

Camels are sweeter than their reputation

The route is 10km (6 miles) one-way and the return journey takes about four hours. A short amble takes you to the northern edge of the village just 1km (²⁄₃ mile) away, where you will come to the Nabatean Temple.

1 Nabatean Temple

An Italian team excavated the ruins of this temple, which was almost completely buried in the sand. It has been dated to Aretas IV in the 1st century AD, and was built on the ruins of an earlier temple to the goddess Allat. The Italians also excavated some prehistoric Bedouin sites here over a six-year period, finishing in 1986. *From here, looking at the right-hand wall of the Rum corridor, you will notice a slight indentation where a few trees are growing, about 800m (¹⁄₂ mile) from the temple ruins. This is the spring called Ain Shellalah.*

2 Ain Shellalah

Leaving your camel, you can scramble over the tumbled rocks of the valley

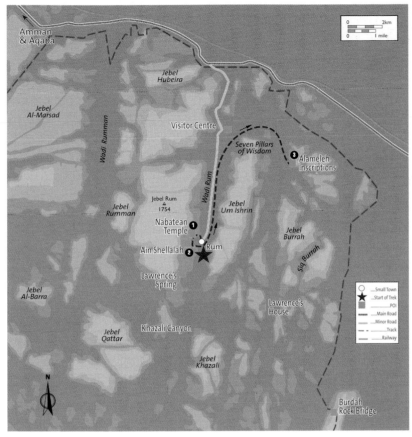

floor up into the crevice itself, where the spring comes out from the rock wall. Beautifully cool and clean to drink, even in the height of summer, this is the most plentiful spring in the Wadi Rum. *Heading north now along the Wadi Rum corridor, you bear right, skirting the mountains to reach an impressive rock face.*

3 Alameleh inscriptions
On this rock face there are excellent examples of ancient rock drawings from prehistoric times, of camels and other wildlife. Thought to be the work of the tribe of Thamud (now extinct), these people came from the town of Al-Hijr in Saudi Arabia, north of Medina. Mentioned in texts as early as the 8th century BC, they were reputed to be a wicked pagan people, later conquered by the Nabateans.

From here the route leads back south through a magnificent area of sand dunes, and skirts round the rocky outcrop to return to Rum village.

Aqaba

A few days spent at Aqaba, Jordan's only window to the sea, enjoying the sandy beaches and the marine life, is an ideal way to relax at the end of a tour round the country. Just 30 minutes' drive from Wadi Rum and 90 minutes' drive from Petra, Aqaba can also be used as a base for exploring the south of the country, and the beach hotels make a wonderful haven to retreat to at the end of a long day of sightseeing.

History

Historically, the port has always been significant. The Bible tells how King Solomon built his fleet here, creating the ships that were to return laden with precious goods like sandalwood and frankincense. The Nabateans of Petra controlled the port, then the Romans, and in Byzantine times it was the seat of a bishop. The medieval town was fortified by walls which can still be seen in places, built by Muslims to make it a safe haven for pilgrims on their way to Mecca. It fell for a short time to the

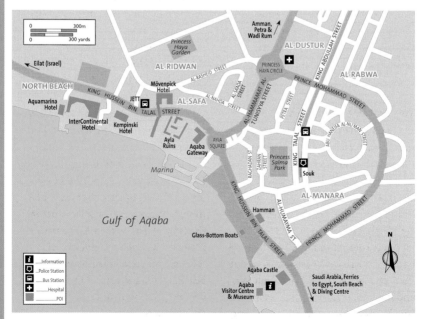

The approach to Aqaba

Crusaders under Raynald of Chatillon, but then Saladin sent in the Egyptian fleet. The Mamelukes built a fort near what is now the modern museum, and in Ottoman times the small garrison was overwhelmed by Arab forces who seized it in 1917 as part of the Arab Revolt.

The well-trodden pass

The name Aqaba means 'mountain pass' in Arabic, a reference to the approach through the mountains for the last few kilometres as you near the sea. The dual carriageway is worn and ridged with the heavy lorry traffic that plies its way ceaselessly up and down the Desert Highway before forking off to the Iraqi border. Ever since the Iran–Iraq war of the 1980s, then after the first Gulf War and now since the US-led invasion of Iraq in 2003, imports destined for Iraq

have been coming in this way to avoid the Persian-Arabian Gulf, vastly increasing the shipping as well as the lorry traffic. On their return they bring back Iraqi oil.

Red Sea rival

As you break through the mountain pass for your first sight of the wonderfully blue sea, the buildings that dominate are actually those of Eilat, Israel's rival resort on the Red Sea, intriguingly close yet distant. Since the 1994 peace treaty, the border has finally been officially opened. Boasting a far more advanced tourist infrastructure, the Israelis have turned Eilat into a major winter sun destination, with monster concrete hotels along the beach. Aqaba has remained mercifully low-rise, and none of its hotels are monsters.

The shoreline at Aqaba is heavily wooded

Aqaba and environs

Aqaba's natural setting is impressive, with the narrow bay ringed by fine mountains and fringed by palm trees. The industrial port area lies round to the east of the town, while the tourist development of 30 or so hotels is mainly to the west, towards the Israeli border.

Pharaoh's Island

This is a full day's excursion by boat and needs to be booked in advance since the island lies within Egyptian territorial waters. The crossing itself only takes an hour but allows plenty of time for swimming offshore before and after lunch, along with an hour or so touring the castle.

The tiny volcanic rock island lies just 250m (820ft) off Egypt's Sinai shore. Known in Crusader times as Isle de Graye, it was built in the 12th century under Baldwin I. The Egyptians claim it as an Islamic citadel built in 1170 by Saladin to defend the Arabian Peninsula from infidel incursions.

Totally restored by the Egyptian Antiquities Organisation in 1986, the castle now boasts a carrier pigeon tower, a tiny mosque, living quarters, and elaborate baths and cisterns. It also has a well-maintained small restaurant prettily set round a man-made sea lagoon where you can swim or paddle. A reef surrounds the island, giving it its other name, Coral Island, and the snorkelling here is far better than anything in Aqaba.

Tours are booked through good middle- and top-range hotels for around JD28 per person. Two days' notice is required to allow time for processing the Egyptian visa.

Seafront

A stroll along Aqaba's landscaped and palm-lined seafront is a pleasant experience. Starting from the luxury hotels at the western end, you can walk for 700m (770yds) to reach the remains of the medieval town, known as **Ayla**, opposite the Aqaba Gulf Hotel. There are still some solid walls with two fine gates, the Syrian and the Egyptian, and finds from the site, abandoned under the Egyptian Fatimids, can be seen in the little Aqaba Museum (*see opposite*).

The promenade continues for another 1km (²/₃ mile) until you reach the pretty little fishermen's harbour, where the day's catch is laid out for sale each evening. Right on the esplanade nearby is the **Aqaba Museum** located inside the **Visitor Centre** (*open: 7.30am–6.30pm (summer), 7.30am–5.30pm (winter); admission charge*), where a mixture of folkloric and archaeological displays is on show. The small fort, called **Aqaba Castle**, is set immediately behind (*open: daylight hours; free admission*). An inscription dates it to the early 16th century and the last of the Mamelukes. It was heavily shelled by the British in World War I.

South Beach

Heading 12km (7¹/₂ miles) out of Aqaba past the fort and industrial port on the road to Saudi Arabia, you will come to this vast sandy beach. Fridays and public holidays get very busy here with picnicking Jordanian families. The setting is very fine, with the steep mountains of Egyptian Sinai opposite, but the real reason to come is the reef, which lies just a short wading distance away (*see 'Coral reefs', pp118–19*). Wear plastic sandals to protect your feet from sea urchins and sharp coral, but otherwise even just goggles will be enough to see the incredibly colourful and rich sea life.
Admission charge.

Aqaba's seafront promenade

Coral reefs

The best of Aqaba's coral reefs are to be found not in front of the luxury hotels but further south at the Yamaniyeh Reef, beyond the industrial port on the road to Saudi Arabia. That is why the popular South Beach, the Royal Diving Centre and the Marine Science Centre Aquarium are located along this coast, 10–15km (6–9 miles) out of the town centre.

Diving and snorkelling are the favourite sports, but for those who don't want to get their feet wet, there is always the option of taking a ride in one of the many glass-bottom boats which run out to the reef, though the experience is nothing like the same. To help with marine-life identification, a visit to the **Aquarium** is recommended (*open: 8am–6pm (summer), 8am–5pm (winter); admission charge*). The most spectacular are sunfish, parrot fish, butterfly fish and balloon fish.

Living coral

Coral consists of a living mass of microscopic creatures that can only

A glass-bottom boat takes non-divers out to the reef

Reef in the Gulf of Aqaba

survive in the water and at very specific temperatures. The places they colonise are where a particular combination of light, warmth and food supply exists, so they attach themselves to hard rock surfaces close to the shore. Once removed from the water they die, so it is completely pointless to break off a piece, imagining it will look equally beautiful once it adorns your living room back home. In any case, the reefs are under threat as it is, battling industrial pollution.

The vast majority of the fish in the Red Sea are harmless, though there are more nasties here than in the Mediterranean. The chances of encountering any and coming to grief are slim, however – far slimmer than having a road accident – so unless you're particularly timid, you shouldn't let the thought of this tiny risk mar your enjoyment of a wonderful environment. Being well informed is never a bad thing though, so below are a few to be aware of.

MARINE PERILS

Stonefish

These ugly fish half bury themselves in the sea bed all around the shore of the Red Sea. They are highly poisonous and well camouflaged, looking rather like greyish-brown stones. Their excruciating sting can be fatal unless the antidote is given, but mercifully the Aqaba hospitals keep the serum. Interim treatment is to bathe the foot in extremely hot water, as hot as you can bear. The safest way to avoid this unlikely but very unpleasant experience is to wear plastic shoes or sandals with hard soles when in the water.

Lionfish

These flamboyant fish are much easier to spot and can therefore be avoided more easily. They swim about rather slowly, are quite large and black and white, with a mane of black-and-white poisonous spines sticking out about 15cm (6in) all round their heads.

Jellyfish

The big ones, especially the purplish Portuguese man-of-war variety, sometimes come in shoals swimming close to shore. It is best to stay out of the water when these are around to avoid their very painful sting. The smaller types just give a sudden burning sensation, but leave no after-effects or marks on the skin.

Getting away from it all

Jordan offers plenty of opportunities to escape such crowds as there are, and even in the busiest sites such as Petra, the area is so vast that it does not take much to get off the beaten track into side valleys where you can again sense the wilderness of the place. Wild areas in secluded spots and those within the popular sites are both described here.

Dana Biosphere Reserve

This 320sq km (124sq miles) nature reserve, tucked away off the King's Highway around 50km (31 miles) north of Petra, is the largest in Jordan and is the country's pioneering ecotourism project, established in 1993. A few days spent here is the ultimate getaway from the 21st century and is highly recommended. Set in the magnificent scenery of Wadi Dana, the reserve is unique in the Middle East. It is a visionary scheme which has transformed the ailing village of Dana and its surroundings into a sustainable community through the efforts of the Royal Society for the Conservation of Nature. Scientific research is also

View down into Wadi Dana

Stumble across Byzantine ruins off the beaten track

conducted here, funded by the World Bank and the UN.

The reserve covers an immense variety of terrain, from peaks of over 1,500m (4,920ft) right down to 50m (165ft) below sea level towards the Dead Sea 14km (9 miles) away. The wildlife includes ibex, mountain gazelle, wolf, red fox, sand cat and at least 215 species of bird, and the diverse ecosystem boasts over 800 species of plant. There are also many archaeological sites within the reserve, some of which are still being excavated by British teams. These range from copper mines dating back 6,000 years that are mentioned in the Bible, to ruined churches and even a Roman tower.

Some 50 Bedouin families live within the reserve, and the villagers' crafts, such as candles, olive-oil soaps, silver jewellery, leather goods and jams, are sold throughout Jordan to help raise money for the local communities.

The reserve's gateway is in the 15th-century stone-built village of Dana, where the **Visitor Centre** (*open: 8am–8pm; tel: 03 227 0497; email: dhana@rscn.org.jo*) will give details of all the hiking trails and arrange a guide and accommodation inside the reserve. The trails range from the one-hour amble of just 1km (²/₃ mile) leading to some caves and Byzantine ruins, which can be done without a guide, to a five-hour trek involving an overnight stay. There are five places to stay in Dana – some in the village, some in the reserve itself – all simple hotels, camps or eco-lodges. The Feynan Wilderness Lodge is lit solely by candles at night,

The landscape around Sabra and Jebel Haroun

giving it a wonderfully intimate atmosphere.

There is a bus from Dana to the village of Qadisiyyeh on the King's Highway; Qadisiyyeh is in turn linked to Tafila further north by minibuses. Admission charge to the reserve.

Jawa

Out in the desert 25km (15¹/₂ miles) east of Dayr Al-Kahf near the Syrian border lie the eerie remains of Jawa, a black basalt town of mysterious origins standing on its own hill. Extensive excavations have been carried out here and the town is thought to have been one of a series of basalt Byzantine cities which continued to thrive under the Umayyad caliphs of Damascus, perhaps because of its proximity to the Arab desert palaces and the pilgrim route to Mecca. But in the mid-8th century the town was destroyed by a severe earthquake, the timing of which

coincided roughly with the fall of the Umayyads and the shift in the centre of power east to Baghdad, so the town lost its role and was not built up again. It lay deserted until the 20th century; a few Druze settlers from the northern Jebel Druze moved in between 1905 and 1909, undertaking some reconstruction; the results were often not identifiably different from the old Byzantine buildings.

Free admission.

Petra

Although Petra receives upwards of 1,500 visitors a day, there are still many parts of the massive 200sq km (80sq mile) site (*see map p90*) where you are virtually guaranteed solitude. The following is a selection of these.

Al-Madras

If you arrive at Petra late afternoon with just a couple of hours of daylight left, this excursion to the cult sanctuary of Al-Madras is an ideal taster which very few people ever try. Buy a two-day pass so you can enter the site proper the next morning without queuing. The path to Al-Madras leads off to the left before entering the Siq, just at the point where the track bends to the right. There is a signpost and the path begins just to the right of the sign, running behind the low stone wall obliquely to the southwest towards a group of rock cliffs. After crossing scrubland you follow the cairns over a rocky area to reach the original rock-cut stairway, badly worn but quite broad. Ten minutes further on, you scramble up one of four connecting staircases to reach the grassy enclosed sanctuary with rock-cut tombs, cisterns, niches and more staircases up to a twin-pooled area with an altar for sacrifices, or 'high place' as these are called in Petra. All around are fabulous views of the distinctive Petra landscape, especially lovely at sunset.

Jebel Haroun and Sabra

This is a whole day's excursion and needs to be done with a guide, taking your own water and provisions. Sabra is a self-contained Nabatean suburb, even having its own rock theatre. It takes two hours from the Qasr Al-Bint area inside the Petra site, either on foot or on horseback. The scenery en route is fabulous as you go through a succession of wadis and past several mountains, including Jebel Haroun with its white sanctuary containing the tomb of the

A tomb at Petra

Prophet Aaron on the summit at 1,396m (4,580ft). To climb this takes a further two hours starting from Qasr Al-Bint, but the path is unclear and a guide is recommended. All but the last 20 minutes can be done on horseback.

The tomb itself was restored by the Mameluke Sultan Qal'aoun in the 13th century, and Greek Orthodox monks lived in it until that time. It is now kept locked and is still venerated as a holy shrine by Muslims and Christians alike. The account of Aaron's death is given in Numbers 20:23–29.

Little Petra

This is another excursion to do if you have your own transport and arrive at Petra too late to enter the site proper, but with a couple of hours of daylight left. Little Petra (also known as Siq Al-Barid) makes a good introduction to Petra, as it is like a miniature suburb, which most people do not visit. The

The Temple at Little Petra

tarmac road is clearly signposted as you start to climb out of Wadi Musa, and runs for 10km (6 miles) to the north. After 2km (1¼ miles), as the road begins to climb, look out on your left for the crumbling remains of Al-Woairah, the major Crusader castle of Petra. Built in the 12th century, its Crusader name was Le Vaux Moise, its Arabic one Wadi Musa, both meaning 'Valley of Moses'.

The tarmac stops at the iron-gate entrance to Little Petra, impressive for its compactness, with three narrow openings leading to three gorges. Everywhere are traces of the Nabatean water system, and steps leading up to mysterious 'high places'. At the end of the third gorge, a final staircase leads up on to an open terrace and out into the adjacent valley, giving a good idea of how these extraordinary valleys are linked through endless series of steps and networks of paths.

Open: daylight hours. Free admission.

Umm Al-Biyarah

From Qasr Al-Bint within the main Petra site, the most challenging and strenuous half-day climb is to Umm Al-Biyarah, the high rock massif that dominates the whole valley of Petra. Very few visitors manage it, and a local guide is advisable as the path is tricky in places and not always clear. A local boy from the refreshments area can generally be found who will be only too happy to assist for a nominal fee. Three hours should be allowed for the return trip

The massif of Umm Al-Biyarah

from Qasr Al-Bint, including about 45 minutes for exploration of the summit.

Part of the ascent has a magnificent rock stairway, the finest in Petra, with a truly processional feel to it as it zigzags upwards. Higher up it is blocked by fallen rocks, and the rest of the climb requires a fair amount of scrambling on all fours up narrow gulleys. On the surprisingly extensive summit are the remains of Petra's original Edomite settlement, dating to the 7th century BC, excavated in the 1960s over a three-year period by a British team whose food and water were delivered by helicopter. From the far western point, the view over the Wadi Araba and Jebel Haroun makes one of the most spectacular volcanic landscapes you are ever likely to see.

Wadi Mujib Reserve

Covering 212sq km (82sq miles) between the King's Highway and the Dead Sea, this nature reserve offers five major hiking trails, including Jordan's best adventure hike, 36km (22 miles) along the Mujib river over two days (*see p81*). All trails must be booked in advance through the Royal Society for the Conservation of Nature (*www.rscn.org.jo*), since admission to the reserve without permission is not allowed.

The reserve's biodiversity is impressive, with the rare Syrian wolf, Blanford's fox, Egyptian mongoose, striped hyena, caracal and many snakes, including the poisonous desert cobra and vipers. There is also an enclosure for the previously endangered Nubian ibex and some of these have been released into the wild. The wadi's scenery is among the most unspoilt and dramatic in Jordan, and it is possible to wilderness camp with advance permission.

When to go

The best times to visit are the spring, particularly March, April and May, and the autumn, specifically September, October and the first half of November. April is probably the best month, before the real heat builds up and while the spring flowers are at their best. Christmas and New Year are also popular. At such times it is essential to book accommodation, especially in places such as Petra, and at the eco-lodges in the Dana Reserve and Azraq, where rooms are limited and there is virtually no other accommodation to fall back on.

Regional variations

Considering how small the country is, the climatic variation is remarkable. Altitude is the main determining factor, with temperatures up on the 1,000m (3,280ft)-high central plateau being lower than elsewhere in summer because of cooling breezes, and much colder in winter due to strong, icy winds that bring frequent snow falls. At the lowest altitudes round the Dead Sea the temperatures are much hotter and more humid, becoming almost unbearable in July and August,

Cacti thrive in the subtropical climate

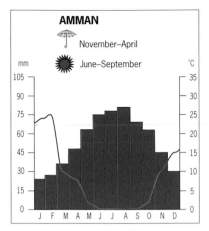

AMMAN

November–April

June–September

mm / °C

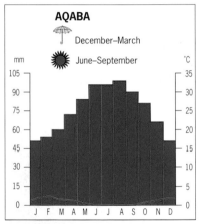

AQABA

December–March

June–September

mm / °C

WEATHER CONVERSION CHART

25.4mm = 1 inch

°F = 1.8 × °C + 32

---

frequently reaching into the 40°C (104°F) range and even higher. In southern Jordan around Aqaba, the Red Sea climate is very benign in the winter months, making swimming in the sea perfectly possible on a day when it may be snowing in Amman.

Aqaba

In trying to keep pace with its Israeli neighbour Eilat, Jordan's Red Sea resort is fast becoming a popular winter destination. In January average temperatures are around 20°C (68°F), so swimming is still feasible, though it is probably at its best in spring and autumn. In summer the sea temperature is more like that of a bath.

Petra

Petra is best avoided in high summer, since some of the climbs can be very punishing under strong sunlight, unless you do them first thing or last thing in the day. The winter months can be wonderful, especially if there are snow falls, turning the whole place into a magical arena. Just make sure you bring a thick pullover or jacket along for the evenings.

Daylight hours

Days can be short in Jordan, and to make the most of your trip early starts are recommended. The sites are at their emptiest first thing in the morning, and so, as well as the heat not having built up, you will also enjoy the atmosphere more. Below are the approximate timings to help your planning:

	Sunrise	Sunset
21 Mar	5.40am	5.45pm
21 June	5.30am	7.45pm
21 Sept	6.30am	6.30pm
21 Dec	6.30am	4.30pm

Getting around

Public transport in Jordan is essentially limited to a very good bus network that links the main cities. However, once you start travelling away from the towns and cities to the various sites such as Jerash, the desert castles, Pella and Umm Qais, hiring a car is the best solution. There is no rail network within the country and the historic Amman–Damascus Hejaz Railway has been suspended for some years now.

By bus/coach

Excellent buses link Amman, from the main bus station at Abdali in the centre of town, to most major towns in Jordan, as well as to Damascus. The national bus company is called **JETT** (*Al-Malek Al-Hussein St, Shmeisani, Amman; tel: 06 566 4146*), and runs efficient services on comfortable, air-conditioned coaches.

For travel to Damascus the best company is called **Challenge** (*Abdali Bus Station; tel: 06 465 4004*), which operates a twice-daily service taking about three or four hours including the border crossing, and costs very little –

Jordan's minor roads are generally deserted

A hatchback car will be good enough to get you to most places

about JD12 return. Sweets and fizzy drinks are offered en route and the coaches are extremely comfortable. At the border there is a chance to get out and stretch your legs, visit the loo and buy a snack or some duty-free goods.

By car
Hire car

The big agencies like Avis, Hertz and Europcar all have offices in Amman and at the airport, and there are also many local firms. The minimum hire period is two days and the driver has to be at least 21. An international driving licence is not essential; your national licence is fine as long as it has a photo. The big firms charge a lot more if you book them in advance through their websites; once you are on the ground they will generally give sizeable discounts. A small vehicle costs around JD25 a day with unlimited kilometres, while hire of 4WD vehicles is a lot more expensive, nearly double the rate of a small car. Make sure you check the exact insurance position, since fully comprehensive coverage is often more expensive and has to be added as an extra. Also, if you have rear-seat passengers, make sure the rear seat belts work properly. The provision of baby seats is a rarity and should not be counted on.

A credit card is used for the deposit. Hire vehicles have green plates, private ones white and government ones red.

A chauffeur-driven car is an alternative for those who feel daunted by the local conditions. The extra cost of this is not too exorbitant, at about JD25 per day to cover the driver's board

Tyre tracks across the desert at Wadi Rum

and lodging. Some drivers are also prepared to act as guides and interpreters, which can be handy.

Private car

You can take your own car into Jordan provided you have obtained a Carnet de Passage from the AA or the automobile club of your country of residence. This permits temporary import into the country for a period of up to three months. Insurance (third-party or comprehensive) is bought at the border. An international licence is advisable but not essential.

Road network

Jordan's road network is one of the best in the Middle East, with motorways and dual carriageways linking Amman with Aqaba in the south and with Irbid and the Syrian border to the north.

Once out of the cities, traffic is generally very light. The small roads are well surfaced and maintained, with very few potholes, making driving in the rural areas quite enjoyable and straightforward. Night driving can be more tricky as a lot of vehicles outside the cities have dodgy lights, so it is best to make sure you complete your itinerary before nightfall, remembering how early darkness falls in the winter months.

By Middle Eastern standards, drivers in Jordan and Amman are relatively competent and well behaved, not least because the driving test is stiff, rather than a mere formality to be settled by a spot of bargaining. Even an eye test is stipulated when the licence comes up for renewal every ten years. Driving is on the right.

Petrol is inexpensive compared with European standards; the smaller cars run on normal benzene, while the middle-sized and upwards need super. Lead-free petrol is still quite rare and generally available only in Amman. Be careful not to let your tank fall below a quarter full when outside the city, as there can sometimes be surprisingly long gaps between garages, such as on the desert circuit for example: the only petrol station in Azraq lies beyond the town on the Iraq road.

By air

The only domestic air service is between Amman and Aqaba, run by Royal Wings, a subsidiary of Royal

Jordanian. It flies daily, takes 45 minutes and costs JD45 one way, a lot faster than the four- or five-hour (for the most part deadly dull) drive down the Desert Highway. From the plane, if you sit on the right-hand side as you fly to Aqaba, you will also enjoy some very fine aerial views over the desert mountains around Wadi Rum.

By taxi

In the towns and cities, yellow taxis are plentiful and reasonably priced, with most fares within Amman costing little more than JD2. Fares are generally rounded up by JD0.2 (or 200 fils). In addition to the standard taxis, there are white *servees* taxis, usually large Peugeots or Mercedes with seven

BY TRAIN

The only passenger railway, from Amman north to Damascus, was part of the original Hejaz railway built in the early 20th century by Turkish soldiers to take pilgrims from Damascus to Mecca. It ran the full length for just six years, till 1914, when it was heavily bombed, but when it was working, it cut the pilgrims' journey time from 50 days on a camel caravan to a mere three hours on the train. The section from Amman to Aqaba is now used only for the transportation of goods, mainly phosphates.

passenger seats, which ply between fixed points beyond the cities. These are not necessarily any faster or less expensive than the buses, and are definitely less comfortable. They do not run to a fixed timetable, but leave when they are full.

Getting around… by camel?

Accommodation

Jordan has the full range of accommodation, from top-class five-star international hotels down to simple one-star places, and now also has a selection of fun new eco-lodges in some of the wilder parts. There is a YMCA in Amman, and wilderness camping is possible anywhere in the desert, except in the Wadi Rum protected area or in the designated nature reserves.

There is very little suitable accommodation, often none at all, in smaller towns such as Madaba, for example, and you should bear this in mind when planning your itinerary. Apart from Amman, Petra and Aqaba, adequate accommodation can be found at Irbid, Ajlun, Azraq, Pella, the Dead Sea, Zerqa Ma'in, Kerak and Wadi Rum.

Top end

The four- and five-star hotels in Jordan are up to full international standard, with chains like the Kempinski, InterContinental, Marriott and Mövenpick, and the luxury hotels on the Dead Sea are recognised as some of the best spa complexes in the world. Listed prices are high, but because there is an oversupply of top-end hotels, especially in Amman, heavy discounts can usually be negotiated which bring prices right down to what you might pay for a three-star equivalent in Europe. Always ask for a discount, and book ahead to get the best reductions.

Middle range

This is the category where there is least accommodation available, as three-star places tend to be few and far between. Amman has a handful, as do Petra and Aqaba, but otherwise there is very little. Jordan no longer has any older hotels of faded grandeur; its last such place, the old 1920s Philadelphia Hotel opposite the Roman amphitheatre in Amman, was rather short-sightedly bulldozed in the 1980s. The preference seems to be for glitz and glamour rather than atmosphere. Among the few exceptions to this are the Taybet Zaman chain in Amman and Petra, which tries to recreate an authentic traditional village atmosphere, and the eco-lodges which are also simple, atmospheric places, but still surprisingly expensive.

Budget

Jordan has no shortage of lower-end accommodation, though the shared facilities make them mostly suited to backpackers and students. Women travelling alone would be best advised to avoid these places altogether.

Seasonal variations

The high season is generally from March to May and from September to October inclusive, when the hotels are at their fullest because the climate is at its best. Obviously if there has been any terrorist incident, thereby leading to mass cancellations, all such considerations go out of the window, and you can negotiate excellent deals. Arab tourists from the Gulf generally come in July and August to escape the heat of their home countries, but since they mostly prefer to stay in self-catering apartments, they do not fill the hotels.

In Aqaba the hotels are at their busiest all winter, from October to April, so their low season is from May to September, when bargains can be negotiated. The luxury Dead Sea hotels have to be booked a long way in advance as they get block-bookings from conference organisers and tour groups, and also a lot of wealthy Amman residents on weekend breaks.

The five-star InterContinental hotel at Aqaba

Accommodation

Food and drink

Food is central to every celebration in Islam. To break food with someone is to seal a friendship, and it is almost a ritual. Eating for eating's sake is considered a private affair, to be done with relaxation in the intimacy of one's own home. For this reason it was regarded as bad form until recent years to eat out in restaurants.

Breakfast

Breakfast is normally available in the hotels from 6.30–10am and generally consists of a buffet-style arrangement with all the usual Western fare like cereals, toast, juices, yogurt, fresh fruit and stewed fruit, but also with plenty of cooked food, such as boiled eggs, omelettes, beef sausages and mashed potatoes. The typical Arab breakfast consists of *fuul* (cold beans) in olive oil, with white cheese, olives and flat Arab bread. Tea and coffee are on offer as the hot drinks. Arabs drink their tea black, so you may have to ask specially for milk, or else use the milk put out in big jugs for the cereals. A selection of sticky pastries and croissants is also often laid out.

Lunch and dinner

Lunch is generally served in Amman restaurants from 1pm to 3pm and dinner after 8pm. Outside the capital, timings are more flexible. Much of the food is bland, international-style cuisine, but Middle Eastern and Jordanian dishes are sometimes on offer. A selection of these is listed below:

Daoud Pasha

This is a meatball stew with onions, pine nuts and tomatoes on rice.

Mansaf

Jordan's national dish is unflatteringly, but quite accurately, nicknamed 'mutton grab'. It is traditionally eaten with the right hand from a large communal platter while sitting on the floor. The meat, usually mutton but occasionally camel, is boiled, cut into chunks and then spread over a huge bed of rice. Sometimes pine nuts and spices are added to enhance the flavour, and a sauce of beaten yogurt and mutton fat may also be poured over to keep it moist. This is the traditional Bedouin feast, prepared for special occasions like weddings or religious holidays. You should not be at all surprised if conversation over this type of food is sparse; an Arabic proverb says, 'When the food is served, the conversation stops.'

Maqlouba

A Palestinian speciality, *maqlouba* is a dish of meat on rice with stewed vegetables, usually aubergine or cauliflower.

Mezze

This is a selection of starters, some hot, some cold, offering tremendous variety and often good value as a main course. The Lebanese do the best *mezze*, but the Jordanian ones are often a close second. Some of the standard cold dishes within the *mezze* are: hummus (chickpea and sesame dip); *baba ghanouj* (simple aubergine dip); *mutabbal* (aubergine dip blended with sesame paste); *fatoush* (Arabic fried bread with salad); *shankleesh* (goat's cheese, onion, pepper and tomatoes); *tahini* (sesame dip); *tabbouleh* (chopped tomato, mint and cracked wheat); and *labneh* (creamy yogurt with walnuts). The hot dishes include *kibbeh* (minced meat in cone shapes stuffed with pine kernels, onion and a kind of cracked wheat known as *burghul*); *fataayir* (thin triangular-shaped pastries filled with cheese or spinach); and falafel (chickpea balls fried in oil).

Mulukhia

This spinach-like vegetable is usually served with stewed lamb. It is sometimes available in the resthouses dotted along the Desert Highway. It was originally more of an Egyptian speciality.

A restaurant in the heart of Petra

Musakhan

This is a West Bank speciality consisting of chicken steamed in olive oil, onions and sumac, then baked on special bread and covered in onions.

Vegetarian options

Jordan, like all Arab countries, is an easy place to be vegetarian, since there are so many freshly prepared starters that are entirely made from vegetables, chickpeas and sesame seeds. This gives a good variety, and for main courses most places offer omelettes. Cheese is rather limited in terms of choice, just being either the white crumbly variety or the processed triangles (the ubiquitous La Vache Qui Rit). Fresh fruit is always in abundant supply.

Jordan grows much of its own fresh produce

Fast food

The Middle East has excellent fast food of its own, served from stands in the *souk* areas or in the town centres. The commonest ones are falafel served in a pitta bread with a little salad inside, making a cheap snack, and *shawarma* (like the Turkish doner kebab), slices of lamb cut thinly from a central rotating roasting spit, also served in pitta bread with salad. In Amman and Aqaba, and now even Petra, there are also the usual American-style hamburger and fried chicken joints, which are far more expensive than the Arab fast food, but wildly popular with wealthy local youths.

Alcohol and soft drinks

Local wines are drinkable, non-vintage reds, whites and rosés, all from the West Bank. Foreign wines are available in good restaurants but are very pricey. The local beer is Amstel and is relatively expensive. *Araq*, the aniseed spirit which goes cloudy when water is added, is the national drink, as in all the Levant. It is 40 per cent proof and smoother than *ouzo*, its Greek counterpart. Drunk with ice and water, it makes an excellent accompaniment to lamb and other greasy dishes. Alcohol is readily available in shops and supermarkets.

Juice stalls, selling freshly squeezed orange, banana, pomegranate and strawberry juice, can be found in downtown Amman and some regional towns, and make a very

The Resthouse terrace at Pella (*see p166*)

refreshing stop in summer. Bottled, still mineral water is cheap and available everywhere, and should be drunk in preference to the tap water. There are several makes, each named after its particular source; the tastes vary slightly.

Shopping for food and drink

Picnic fare can be bought in small local supermarkets in Amman and in most bigger towns. The most convenient things to buy are bread, cheese and tomatoes, plus a few items of fruit like bananas and oranges, and snacks like nuts, dates and salty crisp-like things of

which there is usually a fair selection. For drinks, buy bottles of juice or pop if you want something other than water. Fresh food markets do exist, but are far less in evidence in Jordan than in other Middle Eastern countries.

Tipping

All restaurants of a good standard automatically add 10 per cent service charge to the bill. In a high-quality restaurant it is standard practice to round the bill up slightly as well. In the basic, cheap local eateries, no tip is ever expected, and nothing extra is added to the bill.

Entertainment

The Jerash Festival, with its folkloric music and dancing, is Jordan annual cultural highlight (see p18). Outside the capital of Amman, nightlife in Jordan can really only be found in the big hotels in Aqaba and Petra, which lay on events such as discos and themed nights. Food and eating are a big part of the culture here, and your best bet for an evening's entertainment is generally to enjoy a good meal out.

Keeping yourself entertained

Jordan is basically a country where it is largely up to you to entertain yourself. Local people meet in each other's homes and occasionally gather in restaurants for special occasions, and of course these days large numbers have access to satellite TV so can plug themselves into the endless diet of viewing that is available all round the world. There are also local video/DVD rental stores in the big cities and towns.

The Amman scene

In Amman the free English-language monthly magazine *Jordan Today* can generally be picked up from the reception desk of the big hotels, and gives listings of whatever cultural events may be running. Events are also listed in the English weekly *Jordan Times*.

Cinemas

Amman has a number of modern cinema complexes showing the recent releases (*see 'Directory' listings, p164*). Foreign films are always shown in their original language with Arabic subtitles. Tickets cost around JD5. The downtown cinemas are a bit more basic, generally showing B-grade kung fu and martial arts films, and these are dubbed into Arabic. These venues are heavily dominated by local male youth, with high audience participation levels, so they may not

---

BUY AN APARTMENT

Why not consider buying an apartment in Aqaba? Just hours from Europe and with a year-round warm climate averaging 20°C (68°F) even in January, if you want an affordable place in the sun, the prices here are among the lowest in the region. Jordan has liberal property laws which allow foreigners to buy, and you can go for a flat in town or else buy into one of the Aqaba beachfront developments that are constantly being launched. Some enterprising souls are even starting to see it as the ideal retirement destination and a nice way to while away the winter months. The town has its own airport, so you can fly from Aqaba to visit Egypt as well as various other destinations in the Gulf.

suit Western tastes, especially those of Western women.

Concerts and live shows
Both the Jordanian and foreign cultural centres (*see p164*) in Amman have regular programmes of visiting musicians and performers, the usual venues for which are the public rooms of the big international hotels.

Exhibitions and music
Amman boasts two cultural centres which host concerts and plays, usually in Arabic, and the foreign cultural centres also organise exhibitions, musical performances and lectures by their own visiting nationals. In addition, Amman has a contemporary art exhibition centre and a gallery of fine arts (*see p164*).

Nightclubs
The capital's nightclubs and discos are nearly all to be found in the big international hotels (*see p165*). They are frequented by wealthy local Arabs and it would not be advisable to go there as a single foreign woman, as your presence will be interpreted as availability.

A Nabatean cave has been converted into a bar by Petra's Crowne Plaza Resort Hotel

Shopping

Although Amman has nothing to compare with Damascus, Jerusalem, Aleppo and Cairo's medieval souks (Arab markets), it does have a tradition of Bedouin and Palestinian craftsmanship, and there are a number of outlets in the Jordanian capital where such items can be bought. Gold is also surprisingly cheap.

Souvenirs

The large **four- and five-star hotels** all have souvenir shops, but prices are obviously much higher than in the downtown areas of the capital and tend to be fixed, unless you are buying several items.

At the big sites like **Petra** and **Jerash** there are numerous stalls selling locally made items, a lot of it unbelievably kitsch, like leather camels, sand patterns in bottles and local onyx animals. More worthwhile items are the Bedouin silver jewellery and the Palestinian embroidered robes and clothing, the traditional colouring being the red thread on black. Some items of old brassware and copperware can also still be found, but need to be bargained for to make prices affordable.

In the **Amman** area one of the best and most fun places to buy souvenirs is the **Kan Zaman Village** near the airport. It is a 20-minute drive from the centre of town, and has been designed with flair in a 19th-century restored village. The flagstone streets are lined with shops and boutiques selling goods of high quality, and you can watch items like rugs and jewellery being made. There are also cafés and restaurants constantly supplied with hot bread from traditional ovens.

Another good place in Amman is the **Jordan Design and Trade Center**, opposite the Amman Orchid Hotel in Shmeisani (*open: Sat–Thur 8am–7pm*). It is the showroom for the charity set up by Queen Noor to revive traditional crafts and to create jobs for thousands of women in rural areas. On sale are hand-woven rugs, top-quality pottery, embroidered items and handmade paper. There are other branches at the **Petra Visitor Centre**, the **Jerash Visitor Centre**, at **Aqaba** opposite the fort and in **Madaba** at Haret Jdoudna.

Gold

Downtown Amman has a glittering gold *souk*, and there are gold shops scattered all over Jordan's bigger cities.

Gold is sold by weight, and the prices here are some of the cheapest in the world. The same quality of work and purity of gold outside Jordan costs more than three or four times the Amman price. There are no hallmarks. What you have to look for instead is a stamp that indicates gold purity in parts per thousand; 875 is equivalent to 21 carat and 750 is equivalent to 18 carat. You will be given two receipts when you buy, one for the 'per gram'

market value and another for the cost of the workmanship. Gold merchants have a very strong honour system, so you do not need to worry about being ripped off. Jewels and precious stones, incidentally, are expensive in Jordan and not a good buy, since everything is imported.

Amman souk. *Off King Faisal St in a network of alleys between Cairo Amman Bank and Arab Bank. Open: Sat–Thur 8.30am–7pm.*

Prices in Amman's gold *souk* are among the cheapest in the world

Sport and leisure

Jordan offers many opportunities for adventure sports, such as hiking, rock climbing and camel trekking in Wadi Rum. Most of these activities have to be pre-booked either through local travel agencies like Wild Jordan (see p81) or through local guides in the reserves themselves. On the Red Sea at Aqaba there are plenty of watersports and diving facilities, all of which can be arranged through the hotels. Spa resorts are particularly popular on the Dead Sea, offering the full range of massage and skin treatments.

Football is the national spectator sport, with a Premier League Championship held over the six winter months. Apart from this, popular spectator sports are camel or horse racing at Amman's one racecourse. The massive stadium at Sports City in northern Amman is where Jordan's major sporting events, such as the Pan Arab Games, are held. The deserts and roads are the setting for the two annual car rallies of the 700km (435-mile) **Jordan International Rally** (*www.jordanrally.com*) and for the gruelling 50km (31-mile) **Amman–Dead Sea Marathon**, which takes runners to the 'lowest point on Earth'.

Aerosports

Based at Aqaba airport, the **Royal Aero Sports Club** (*Tel: 03 205 8050. www.fly.to/rpacj*) is one of the leading clubs of its type in the Middle East. Using two-seater microlight planes, you can take a range of sightseeing trips, from simple 20-minute outings around

the bay for JD25, to flights to Wadi Rum costing JD300 for five passengers, offering unparalleled views over the desert and mountains. Also on offer is tandem paragliding from 3,000m (9,800ft), as well as 90-minute hot-air balloon rides over Wadi Rum at dawn.

In Amman the **Royal Jordanian Gliding Club** (*Tel: 06 489 1401*) based at Marka airport offers free-flying or motorised glide rides above the capital for a mere JD20 an hour.

Climbing

Wadi Rum offers some serious rock climbing for enthusiasts, with challenging cliffs and canyons. Full details are given in Tony Howard's book *Treks and Climbs in Wadi Rum, Jordan* (Cicerone, 2007), which rates all climbs according to difficulty. Climbs here can be undertaken all year round, which is handy when the European climbing season is over. There are locally trained guides who can accompany you. A few of the easier climbs, such as the Rock

Bridge at Burdah (*see p109*), can be done by those with no specific training, but a certain level of fitness and agility is still required.

Walking and trekking

Thanks to the **Royal Society for the Conservation of Nature** (*PO Box 1215, Amman 11941. Tel: 06 533 7931. www.rscn.org.jo*), walking and trekking are now becoming popular pastimes. At both the Dana Biosphere Reserve (*see pp120–22*) and the Wadi Mujib Reserve (*see pp80–81*), there are now marked footpaths with routes varying from just an hour or two to whole days. Within the conservation area of Wadi Rum there are now also set routes for a selection of treks in the desert ranging from one hour to overnight, as well as camel treks, which can last for just an hour or two, to overnight or even up to seven days for those who want a real dose of desert lifestyle.

Watersports

All diving and snorkelling is based at Aqaba; there are several professional dive centres based along the 27km (17 miles) of coastline between the town and the Saudi border. The Aqaba hotels also offer waterskiing, windsurfing and pedalos from their beaches.

A pool with a view at Petra's Crowne Plaza hotel

Children

Like all Arabs, Jordanians love children and they are welcomed everywhere in hotels and restaurants. Jordanian children are allowed to stay up late with their parents at restaurants and are very indulged by Western standards, yet it is rare to see a Jordanian child misbehaving or having a tantrum. With eating habits too, they are simply expected to eat smaller quantities of whatever their parents have ordered, rather than have special food prepared, so food problems do not arise and 'fussy eaters' are unheard of.

Babies

Very young children can be carried around in backpacks without difficulty, and the abundance of baby food that can simply be mixed with mineral water from packets makes feeding easy. Juices of all flavours are available and can be diluted to taste.

Toddlers

Toddlers are much more difficult as they will not be able to cope with the long distances of walking involved in places like Petra or Jerash, and the terrain is not suitable for pushchairs. With a toddler you can, however, enjoy a beach holiday at Aqaba or on the Dead Sea.

Older children

The best age of child for a holiday in Jordan is definitely the over-ten group. They will usually have the strength and energy to cope with the long walking distances and get huge enjoyment out of clambering over the **Crusader**

castles (*see p88*) and going on the walking and camel treks at **Wadi Rum** (*see pp112–13*). And they will remember the experience, unlike the little ones, who often won't. They will also enjoy watching the ostriches and oryx at the **Shaumari Wildlife Reserve** (*see p63*), and staying in the candlelit eco-lodges of the **Dana Biosphere Reserve** (*see pp120–22*). Children who like beaches and water will have great fun at the **Dead Sea** (*see pp74–5*), messing about on pedalos and floating, and at **Aqaba** the younger ones can observe the coral reefs from a glass-bottom boat (*see pp118–19*), while the older ones try a bit of snorkelling.

Hotels

Many hotels offer rooms with three beds so a child can stay in the same room as his or her parents. The buffet feeding arrangements that many of the bigger hotels offer at breakfast, lunch and dinner also make eating straightforward, as there is bound to be something that appeals from the range, and quantity is not a problem as they can keep going back for more of their favourite thing. The big hotel chains all have swimming pools and most have tennis courts and playgrounds.

Precautions

The main precautions for children of all ages are to do with the heat and the sun. Always ensure they are well protected from the sun as 80 per cent of all skin damage occurs before the age of 20, and make certain they wear high-factor sun creams. Best of all is to keep them out of the direct sun between 11am and 3pm, unless you are at the Dead Sea, where UV rays are naturally filtered and therefore harmless. If you are travelling in your own hired car make sure you always have plenty of water and juices handy, as well as non-meltable snacks like nuts and crisps.

Children see the ancient sites as giant playgrounds

Essentials

Arriving

By air

Amman has two international airports: Queen Alia International Airport, which takes all the intercontinental traffic, and Marka Airport, which is used for shorter regional flights within the Middle East. Buying visas on arrival is straightforward and quick. Queen Alia has two terminals, with one on either side of the road. Terminal 1 is primarily used by Royal Jordanian and Terminal 2 mainly by the other carriers.

Once outside, there are always taxis waiting. The correct metered fare into the city centre (a 45-minute drive away) will be around JD15–18, though many taxi drivers will try to tell you the set fare is JD25 or more. Check that the meter is on zero when you start off, as it is a common trick with gullible foreigners to already have the meter set on a figure before you even set off. Baggage does not cost extra. To avoid the hassle you can simply go to the airport taxi office to the left in the arrivals area and pay the official fixed fare in return for a slip which you then hand to the taxi driver. There are several car-hire companies with offices in the arrivals area, so you can compare rates to find the best deal.

Royal Jordanian arrivals and departures. Tel: 06 445 3200. www.rj.com
Other carriers' arrivals and departures. Tel: 06 445 2700.

By sea

There are two passenger ferries which arrive at Aqaba on the Red Sea from the Egyptian port of Nuweiba. They run daily and the fast service takes about an hour, while the slower car-ferry journey lasts four or five hours. Avoid the *hajj* (pilgrimage) time before Eid Al-Adha (around 6–9 Nov 2011, 26–29 Oct 2012, 15–18 Oct 2013), when the ferries get packed with pilgrims returning home from Mecca to Egypt. If you want to leave Jordan this way, Egyptian visas can be bought on entry.

Arab Bridge Maritime Company. Tel: 03 209 2000. www.abmaritime.com.jo

By land

There are two border crossings between Syria and Jordan and both are efficiently run and relatively straightforward. You should allow anything from 20 minutes to an hour for the border formalities, depending on how busy the crossing is, which varies from day to day. Fridays and public holidays are often the busiest times. The border posts are open 24 hours.

Comfortable air-conditioned coaches are run by two companies: the Jordanian one, **JETT**, and the Syrian one, **Challenge**, which is cheaper, costing just JD12 return (Amman–Damascus) if bought from the Jordanian end and the equivalent of JD8 return if bought in Syria. The trip takes about four hours including the border crossing, and you are given free soft drinks and sweets. There are two departures a day, usually at around 8am and 3pm.

The other way of crossing by land is by *servees* taxis. These leave from the bottom end of Abdali bus station and run day and night as and when they fill up. They are a bit more expensive than the coach but are often a little quicker, especially at the border where they provide customs with fewer people to process.

JETT (Jordanian Express Travel & Tourism). Al-Malik Al-Hussein St, Shmeisani, Amman. Tel: 06 566 4146. Challenge. Abdali bus station, Amman. Tel: 06 465 4004. Fax: 06 465 4005.

By train

Very few people use the old Hejaz Railway to cross to Syria, not least as it is currently suspended. Even when it does run, it is very slow and only leaves twice a week. It uses the charming old station on King Abdullah I St, 2.5km (1¹/₂ miles) east of Raghadan station in Amman.

Departs on Monday and Thursday at 8am. Ticket office. Tel: 06 489 5413. Open: from 7am. Check www.seat61.com for latest information.

Departing

The airport is clearly marked from Amman city centre, and lies 35km (22 miles) to the south, just off the Desert Highway. The taxi fare is about JD15 and you should allow about

45 minutes for the drive. If you are flying Royal Jordanian it is a good idea to use their **City Terminal** check-in service at the 7th Circle (*open: 7.30am–10pm*). You can check in your bags here between 24 and 3 hours before your flight, and even get an extra baggage allowance of 15kg. From here they run a private bus direct to the airport every 30 minutes for just JD3, and then on arrival you go straight through a fast-track gate and direct to passport control. After that you can head up the escalator to the duty-free shop, which sells a range of last-minute presents like sweet pastries, traditional ceramics and worry beads.

The departure tax for those crossing the Syrian border by coach has recently been scrapped. For those departing by air, it is already included in the cost of the ticket.

Customs

On arrival you may buy 200 cigarettes, 1 litre of spirits and 2 litres of wine at the duty free. Expensive goods such as cameras may be subject to duty but only if the customs officials suspect you may sell it while in Jordan. Any items considered pornographic (e.g. magazines, DVDs) will be confiscated as potentially corrupting. There are no restrictions on the import and export of currency.

Electricity

The supply in Jordan is 220V, 50Hz, the same as in Europe. Power cuts are rare and the supply is stable. In new buildings and the big hotels, the plug sockets take the British-style square three-pin plug, but older buildings have circular two- or three-pin sockets; visitors should bring a universal adaptor to cover all options.

Email and Internet

Internet cafés are springing up all over the place. You can pop in and check your emails for a few fils as long as you have an account which can be accessed internationally, such as Hotmail or Yahoo. The bigger hotels also have business centres where you can do this, though their rates are higher and access may be limited to standard office hours. If you are carrying your own laptop make sure you have a UK–US adaptor, since the wider British-style phone plug sockets are only found in newer buildings. The big 5-star hotels generally have access points in the rooms.

Etiquette and body language

Always dress conservatively, especially if you're a woman, covering arms to below the shoulders and legs to the knee, and you should experience no hassles. Eye contact with men should be kept to a minimum, otherwise there is a risk it will be misinterpreted as romantic encouragement. As a woman, do not offer your hand to be shaken first as this is seen as too forward and provocative. If, as a Western woman, your behaviour and demeanour convey availability, you will undoubtedly be hassled by local men.

Public displays of affection between men and women are not socially acceptable, whether they are married or not. Even walking hand in hand is seen as distasteful and unnecessarily demonstrative. Homosexuality is very taboo, though there is a small underground gay scene in Amman, but nothing compared to Tel Aviv, Beirut or Cairo. Contact between members of the same sex is, however, totally acceptable in Arab culture; men can walk hand in hand and kiss each other on the cheek quite openly, as can women provided it is not in a romantic way.

Both genders should avoid pointing at something with the index finger as this is thought to cast the evil eye. Showing the soles of your feet while sitting is also regarded as insulting to those around you, and eating from a communal plate should be with the right hand only, the left hand being used for toilet ablutions.

Money

Jordan seems expensive compared to Egypt or Syria, but in comparison to Israel or to European prices, it is still good value. The biggest regular dent in your budget is likely to be made by entry fees (*see p92*), especially to the major sites like Petra and Jerash. Hotel prices in Petra are also very inflated compared to the rest of the country.

Currency

The unit of currency is the Jordanian dinar, abbreviated as JD, and even in Arabic this is expressed phonetically as 'jaydee' instead of 'dinar'. It is pegged against the US dollar and the latest rates can be checked at *www.oanda.com*. The *dinar* is subdivided into either 1,000 *fils* or 100 piastres and, whether written or spoken, it appears to be entirely random which of these is used.

The banknotes come in JD50, JD20, JD10, JD5 and JD1. They have Arabic on one side and English on the other, so there is no confusion as to which is which. Try to avoid having JD50 or JD20 banknotes since these can be difficult to change other than at hotels or expensive restaurants. There are four common coins: the distinctive half dinar, which is gold-coloured, seven-sided and with a circular central silver inset; the quarter dinar, which is similar but smaller and without the silver inset; and coins of ten and five piastres, both of which are thin, round and silver. All the coins do state their value in English somewhere, but usually hidden away in tiny writing.

Changing money

You can buy Jordanian currency from a bank in the West before travelling, and if you are organised you can order at least JD50 worth to cover the initial visa and taxi costs. If you can, it will be worth your while to bring all the Jordanian currency with you that you anticipate needing, as this will save you the higher Jordanian commission rates and the hassle of changing money on arrival. There are no currency restrictions on import or export, so you do not have to worry about overstepping any limit. Theft is very rare in Jordan so you need not be unduly concerned about carrying large amounts of cash around. Entrance fees for sites like Petra and Jerash must be in cash and JD; credit cards are not accepted, even when the amount is very high.

Banks have limited opening hours, but in bigger towns there are usually exchange bureaux where the rate is fractionally better anyway. Unlike in other Middle Eastern countries where US dollars can be used and are often preferred by local traders, in Jordan the preference is for their own currency. Traveller's cheques are an expensive way of carrying money, the procedure for changing them can be long-winded and the exchange rate is generally lower than for cash.

ATMs

Banks in Amman and the larger towns all have ATMs which are easy to use and function 24 hours a day. There tends to be a daily withdrawal limit of JD100 or JD300. Make certain you have a PIN that will work overseas before relying entirely on this method.

Credit and debit cards

These are widely accepted in Jordan's bigger hotels, better licensed restaurants
(*Cont. on p152*)

Language

Written Arabic is known as *fus-ha* and is the same from one Arab country to another, meaning that an Iraqi newspaper can be read in Morocco with no problem. Spoken Arabic, on the other hand, varies considerably from country to country and is known as *aamiya*. An Algerian, for example, would be largely unintelligible to a Lebanese and vice versa. Jordanian spoken Arabic is loosely related to Palestinian, Syrian and Lebanese versions, though there are notable differences. The following transliterated words and phrases represent the Jordanian form of the language. *See also p156.*

GREETINGS

English	Jordanian Arabic
Hello (literally 'Peace be upon you')	assalaamu alaykum
Hello (response: 'And on you the peace')	wa alaykum assalaam
Hello, welcome	marhaba
Goodbye	ma'a assalaama

USEFUL WORDS AND PHRASES

English	Jordanian Arabic
Please go ahead (e.g. host inviting you inside, or to start eating)	tafaddal (to a male) *or* tafaddalee (to a female)
If God wishes (i.e. hopefully)	in sha Allah
Praise be to God (expression of relief)	al-hamdu lillah
Yes	na'am *or* aiwa
No	laa
Please	min fadlak
Thank you	shukran
Sorry, excuse me	muta'assif
Hurry up, let's go	yallah
More, again, also	kamaan
Is it possible? May I?	mumkin?
No problem	mish mushkila
Never mind	ma'a laysh
Forbidden	mamnou'
Good	kuwayyis

English	Jordanian Arabic	English	Jordanian Arabic
Bad	mish kuwayyis	Breakfast	futoor
Today	al-yawm	Lunch	ghada
Tomorrow	bukra	Dinner	'ashaa
How much (cost)?	Bikaam? or adaysh?	Glass	kubbayeh
		Wine	nabeedh
Cheap	rakhees	White wine	nabeedh abyad
Expensive	ghaali	Red wine	nabeedh ahmar
Money	fuluus	Beer	bira
A lot, much, more	kateer	Mineral water	moi ma'daniyah
Open	maftuuh	Tea	shay
Closed	musakker or mughlaq	Coffee	gahwa
		Eggs	bayd
Shop	dukkaan	Fish	samak
Bank	bank or masraf	Meat	lahma
Chemist	saydalia	Fruit	fawakeh
Diarrhoea	ishaal	Milk	haleeb
Market	souq	Butter	zibda
Museum	mathaf	Cheese	jibneh
Hospital	mustashfaa	Yogurt	laban
Police	shurta	Jam	murabba
Airport	mataar	Honey	'asl
Ticket	tadhkara	Bread	khubz
Hotel	otel or funduq	Sugar	sukkar
Room	ghurfa	Vegetables	khudra
Suitcase	shanta	Shared taxi	servees
Toilet, bathroom	hammam or bait moi	Car	sayyaara
		Right	yameen
Towel	manshafa	Left	yasaar or shimaal
Soap	saabuun	Straight on	dughri or 'ala tool
Gents	rijaal		
Ladies	sayyidaat	Far	ba'eed
Restaurant	mat'am	Near, close by	gareeb
The bill	al-hisaab	Petrol	benzene
Hot	harr	Where?	wayn?
Cold	baared	Bus	baas

and upmarket shops. Visa is the most commonly accepted card. You may find, however, that your bank imposes a handling charge, and of course the exchange rate may not be favourable. Avoid using a credit card for a cash advance from an ATM as this will incur hefty interest charges.

Opening hours

Archaeological sites are usually open from 8am to dusk every day.
Banks are open 8.30am–12.30pm and sometimes again 4–5.30pm, and are closed on Fridays.
Government departments open 8am–2pm, and are closed on Fridays and Saturdays.
Museums are usually open 9am–5pm and closed on Fridays.
Shops in town centres open from 8 or 9am to 8 or 9pm every day, but most will close for a couple of hours on Fridays over the noonday prayer period.

Passports and visas

It is a good habit to carry your passport with you at all times in case of checkpoints or accidents. Make sure you also have a photocopy of your passport details, kept somewhere separately, in case of loss or theft.

All foreigners entering Jordan need a visa. These can be bought on arrival at the border crossing if you are arriving by land, or at the airport if by air. Your passport must be valid for at least six months beyond the date of entry. The standard fee for a visa is JD20 for single

entry. This must be paid in JD and there are money-changing facilities if you have only foreign currency, or you can use an ATM. The airport rate is not that good, so you may prefer to change just a small amount here then change more at a city-centre bank. All tourist visas are valid for 30 days. If you intend to stay longer you must register with the police at any police station to extend your visa for up to three months. There is no charge for this and the process takes just a few minutes. If you arrive at Aqaba, you are given a special free 30-day visa, but it is more difficult to extend this.

Pharmacies

These are plentiful in all cities and towns and are well stocked with all the usual toiletries. Prescription drugs can often be bought over the counter after a chat with the pharmacist, whose English is generally very good. Items such as condoms, tampons and pads are always stocked.

Post

Postcards and airmail letters sent from Jordan take a surprisingly long time to arrive in Western Europe – around two weeks – and up to a month to arrive in

RAMADAN

In the Muslim holy month of Ramadan, shops, museums and offices have shortened hours, generally closing at 2 or 3pm. The big tourist sites like Petra and Jerash will be unaffected, but at the smaller sites the guardians may pack up early and go home.

the USA or Australasia. Stamps cost between 300 and 500 fils and can often be bought at shops where the postcards are sold, with a small mark-up, but it beats queuing at the post office. Posting is best done at your hotel, as the street postboxes are only randomly emptied.

Public holidays

The weekend is Friday, when the archaeological sites, parks and nature reserves get very crowded with picnicking families or huge groups of schoolchildren on outings.

Fixed annual public holidays

1 January	New Year's Day
30 January	King Abdullah's Birthday
22 March	Arab League Day
1 May	Labour Day
25 May	Independence Day
9 June	Accession of King Abdullah
10 June	Army Day and Anniversary of the Great Arab Revolt
14 November	King Hussein Remembrance Day
25 December	Christmas Day

Religious holidays

These move 11 days earlier each year according to the lunar calendar. In addition to the Muslim holidays listed below, Good Friday is celebrated.

Prophet's Birthday	4 Feb 2012, 24 Jan 2013
Start of Ramadan	20 Jul 2012, 9 Jul 2013
Eid Al-Fitr	19–21 Aug 2012, 8–10 Aug 2013
Eid Al-Adha	6–9 Nov 2011, 26–29 Oct 2012, 15–18 Oct 2013
Muslim New Year	26 Nov 2011, 15 Nov 2012, 5 Nov 2013

Smoking

Smoking is deeply ingrained among Arab men, and even though it is in theory banned in public places, this is loosely enforced. Everyone is assumed to smoke, and in *servees* taxis, for example, it is normal for your fellow passengers to smoke all over you, closing the windows against the draught. If you are a non-smoker, this may make travel by air-conditioned coach preferable, where smoking is not permitted.

Suggested reading and media

Books

The best modern guides on the country's history are *History of Jordan* by Philip Robins (Cambridge University Press, 2004), which covers right up to the first few years of King Abdullah's reign, and *The Modern History of Jordan* by the leading Lebanese historian Kamal Salibi (IB Tauris, 1998), which details the period from the Arab Revolt up to the first Gulf War.

For interesting biographies that also give a flavour of life in Jordan there is Queen Noor's *Leap of Faith: Memoirs of an Unexpected Life* (Miramax, 2003), King Hussein's *Uneasy Lies the Head* (Heinemann, 1962) and Glubb Pasha's *A Soldier with the Arabs* (Hodder & Stoughton, 1957).

For a flavour of the region through literature you might try Mahmoud Darwish's *Memory for Forgetfulness: August, Beirut, 1982* (University of California Press, 1995), a collection of prose poems by the greatest Palestinian poet. Finally, of course, Jordan is the perfect setting for T E Lawrence's *Seven Pillars of Wisdom* (Anchor, 1991).

Other English-language media

There is an English daily, the *Jordan Times*, and a weekly, *The Star*, a fun magazine published on Mondays. Radio Jordan (96.3 FM) broadcasts in English and there is also the BBC World Service (103.1 FM in Amman and 1323 AM in the rest of the country). In the hotels most satellite services receive CNN and a couple of Western film channels.

Sustainable tourism

Thomas Cook is a strong advocate of ethical and fairly traded tourism and believes that the travel experience should be as good for the places visited as it is for the people who visit them. That's why we firmly support The Travel Foundation, a charity that develops solutions to help improve and protect holiday destinations, their environment, traditions and culture. To find out what you can do to make a positive difference to the places you travel to and the people who live there, please visit *www.makeholidaysgreener.org.uk*

Tax

A VAT-type tax of 16 per cent is added to bills in mid- and upper-range hotels and restaurants, and a compulsory service tax of 10 per cent is also often added at the better establishments. These taxes can often give a nasty shock, boosting your bill by over 25 per cent.

Telephones

The phone network is run by Jordan Telecom, and has recently been privatised.

To call Jordan from overseas, dial the country code (*962*), followed by the area code minus the initial zero, then the local number.

Within the country all land lines have a two-digit area code, followed by a seven-digit number. There are just four area codes: *02* for north Jordan; *03* for south Jordan; *05* for the Jordan Valley and the east of the country; and *06* for the Amman area.

Useful phone numbers

In-country Directory Enquiries *1212* or *06 464 0444*
International Directory Enquiries *1213*
Operator *1322*

Mobile phones

Jordanian mobile-phone numbers have eight digits with a *07* prefix. If your own mobile works on the GSM system, as most mobiles in the UK, Australia and New Zealand do, it will work fine in Jordan, and all you have to do is make sure you have international roaming set up. Texting is by far the cheapest way of staying in touch with friends and family abroad, and avoids the heavy charges of overseas phoning.

If you are staying for long enough to make it worthwhile, or plan to visit regularly, a surprisingly cheap option is to buy a Jordanian handset for about JD50 from either Fastlink or MobileCom, which have shops all over the big cities. You then buy a pre-pay call plan over the counter and within ten minutes you are set up with your own Jordanian mobile, SIM card and phone number.

Time differences

Jordan is usually GMT +2 hours, and goes on to daylight saving time at the beginning of April until the end of October, though the dates are not fixed and do not coincide exactly with the European times. This means that for a short time in the spring Jordan can be 3 hours ahead of London, and just 1 hour ahead for a short time in the autumn. Comparative times in other countries for most of the year are as follows:

Australia 7 hours ahead of Jordan
Canada 7 hours behind Jordan
New Zealand 10 hours ahead of Jordan
South Africa same as Jordan
United Kingdom 2 hours behind Jordan
United States (east coast) 7 hours behind Jordan.

Toilets

While public toilets are a rarity in towns, they do exist at sites, usually at the entrance. In cities and towns, restaurant loos can be used without difficulty.

When you do use a public toilet, you'll find it isn't too bad as long as it's manned by a cleaning attendant proffering toilet paper or tissues. 50 fils is fine as a tip. There is often a choice between the hole-in-the-ground variety and the conventional sit-down style, but whichever it is, always put your used toilet paper in the little basket, never down the toilet, otherwise it will become blocked.

Travellers with disabilities

Jordan is not well geared up for travellers with disabilities, and those with limited mobility are best advised to make sure they travel with a tour group that is aware of the problem and can make necessary arrangements in advance. Wheelchair access to hotels, restaurants and public buildings is virtually non-existent, and pavements in towns are narrow and uneven with high kerbs.

Petra is potentially the only site where a visit is possible, by hiring a horse-drawn carriage to take you right down through the Siq to the Qasr El-Bint area. From there, by prior arrangement, it is possible to be picked up by car and driven through a checkpoint back to your hotel via the Wadi Turkmaniyeh.

The Arabic language

To many Westerners, Arabic is a language that looks like an incomprehensible series of squiggles and dots, and sounds like an equally incomprehensible series of gutturals and hisses. It is, however, actually a subtle and expressive language, beautiful in the way that French is widely regarded to be. By the very nature of its structure, Arabic is an extremely rich language, capable of expressing fine shades of meaning, and this is reflected in the wealth of Arabic literature, especially poetry. The average English tabloid reader is said to have a working vocabulary of 3,000 words, whereas the Arab equivalent is said to have about 10,000.

the right-to-left flow of text. Yet the script is in fact the easiest thing about Arabic. The alphabet contains 29 letters and there are strict rules to determine which characters join on to which. And unlike most European languages, there are no exceptions to these rules. The characters change their shape according to their position within the word but always within the same rules. The process of learning the characters and their shapes is a memory exercise which can be easily done in a few days and thereafter just requires practice. As to the right-to-left text direction, it simply takes a little time to adjust, like driving on the right instead of on the left.

Script

Non-Arabic speakers are generally daunted above all by the script and

Hidden vowels

Having mastered the script, the task begins in earnest. The first difficult

Bilingual signs are the norm in Jordan

Arabic inscription above Qasr Azraq

thing you now encounter is that only the consonants are written, and that you have to supply the vowels yourself. How do you know which vowels to put where? The answer is that you do not, or at least not until you have a thorough grasp of Arabic grammar and word structure, something which generally takes a minimum of three or four months' study. For this reason, all beginners' texts and children's schoolbooks are fully annotated with vowel signs added in the form of dashes and dots above and below the line. Getting a student to read an un-vowelled text aloud is always an excellent way, therefore, of assessing his or her level, since it instantly reveals the depth of understanding of Arabic.

Pronunciation

This is another area which is not as daunting as it may seem. Of the 29 consonants, 18 have direct phonetic equivalents in English, such as b, d, t, l, m and s. The rest have no direct equivalent and range

from emphatic versions of d, s, t and h to a small handful of sounds which are difficult for Westerners to pronounce. The guttural stop, usually represented in transliteration as a reversed comma, and called *'ain* in Arabic, is probably the one that gives most trouble.

Root system

Like Hebrew, Arabic is a Semitic language with a root system. The root of an idea or concept is represented by a simple verb, usually consisting of three consonants. These verbs are the very basis of the Arabic language, and all variations of meaning around the root idea are expressed by imposing different patterns on the basic verb root. For example, from the verb root *ktb* (*kataba* when vowelled) which means 'he wrote', you can make *maktab* meaning 'office', *maktaba* meaning 'library' and *kitaab* meaning 'book'. The verbs are fully conjugated so *katabnaa* means 'we wrote' and *yaktabuuna* means 'they are writing'.

Emergencies

Emergency phone numbers
Ambulance *193*
Fire *199*
Police *191*

Consulates and embassies
The usual opening hours are
Sunday–Thursday 9am–noon.
Australia *41 Kayed Al-Armouti St.*
Abdoun Al-Janoubi. Tel: 06 580 7000.
www.jordan.embassy.gov.au
Canada *Pearl of Shmeisani Building,*
Abdalhameed Shoman Street, Shmeisani,
Amman. Tel: 06 566 6124.
www.jordan.gc.ca
New Zealand *99 Al-Malek Al-Hussein*
St, Downtown Amman. Tel: 06 463 6720.
Fax: 06 463 4349. www.mfat.govt.nz
South Africa *15 Al-Bashir Al-Shuwaiqi,*
North West Abdoun, Amman. Tel: 06
592 1194.
UK *Dimashq St, Wadi Abdoun, Abdoun,*
Amman. Tel: 06 590 9200.
http://ukinjordan.fco.gov.uk
USA *20 Al-Umawiyeen St, Abdoun,*
Amman. Tel: 06 590 6000.
http://jordan.usembassy.gov

Crime and safety
As in most Arab countries, street crime is
rare and assaults, rapes, muggings and
pickpocketing are far less common here
than in Western cultures. This is because
the honour system is deeply ingrained
and shame would be brought on the
family by the perpetrator. Tourist police
are posted at all tourist sites throughout
the country to deal with any problems
that arise, and they speak good English.
It is best to avoid downtown Amman on
Fridays in case of demonstrations by pro-
democracy groups. Terrorist incidents are
rare and you would have to be extremely
unlucky to get caught up in any such
episode; your chances are certainly no
higher in Jordan than in your own home
country. Drugs are not prevalent, and the
use of hashish is regarded as beyond the
pale by Jordanians. There are severe
penalties for anyone caught trafficking
drugs, and Jordanian jails are notoriously
unpleasant even by Middle Eastern
standards. Homosexuality is not illegal
per se, but should be kept discreet.

Healthcare
Medical facilities in Jordan are generally
pretty good (especially in Amman), but
for a carefree holiday, invest a little
time in planning, and make sure you
have adequate health insurance.
Prevention is the best option, so
make sure your vaccinations are up
to date. The following are advised:
diptheria and tetanus (lasts ten years);
hepatitis A (lasts one year); polio
(ten years); measles, mumps, rubella
(check you had your booster);
typhoid (if travelling for more than
a fortnight); yellow fever (only
needed if you are arriving from an
infected area).

Take care in the sun if there's little cover, such as here in the Jordan Valley

Health risks

The sun is likely to be your biggest health risk, easily avoided by simply staying out of the fierce midday rays, keeping your head covered and being sure to wear plenty of high-factor sun cream. Be particularly careful in the hotter summer months. Apart from that, you are advised to drink only bottled water and to travel with anti-diarrhoeal drugs just in case you eat something which disagrees with you.

Police

Jordan maintains an efficient and helpful police force. Also, at all major tourist sites there are highly visible tourist police wearing armbands with English writing, partly as a deterrent for any potential terrorist attack, partly to instil confidence in visiting tourists.

Directory

Accommodation price guide

The price ratings in this book are based on a double room with breakfast including taxes, and are the high season prices. As there is an oversupply at the top end, especially in Amman, most of the time these can be negotiated down by asking for a discount, and while this can be done on the spot, you will usually get a better deal by negotiating in advance of your stay online or by phone.

£	under JD30
££	JD30–60
£££	JD60–100
££££	over JD100

Eating out price guide

Prices are based on an average meal without drinks, including taxes. Local wine costs around JD14–16 a bottle, while foreign wine costs JD30–40 a bottle. Spirits cost JD3–5 a measure.

£	under JD6
££	JD6–12
£££	JD12–20
££££	over JD20

AMMAN

ACCOMMODATION

There are no campsites in or near Amman.

Amman Palace ££

Seventy large though somewhat run-down rooms near the *souk* district. There's air conditioning and satellite TV, but the hot-water supply in the en-suites can be temperamental. *Saqf Sayl, near the Church of the Saviour, Downtown. Tel: 06 464 6172. Email: aplchotl@ hotmail.com*

Canary ££

Quiet family hotel with 21 clean en-suite rooms, and canary cages in the mini-garden. Breakfast is served, but the hotel doesn't have a restaurant. *Opposite the Terra Sancta College, Jebel Weibdeh. Tel: 06 463 8353. Fax: 06 465 4353. Email: canary_h@hotmail.com*

Manar ££

Very good value in the summer when it is the cheapest place by far and also offers a swimming pool. The 72 rooms are a little past their best but

do have en-suite facilities. Restaurant, coffee shop and bar. *Al-Shareef Abdul Hamid Sharaf St, Shmeisani. Tel: 06 566 2186. www.almanarhotel.com. Email: manarhotel-amman@wanadoo.jo*

Hisham £££

In a quiet, leafy embassy suburb, the 22 rooms are comfortable and spacious, if a little run-down. Friendly and helpful staff, simple restaurant and pleasant outdoor garden seating in summer. Popular with journalists

and diplomats on a lower budget. Car hire and business services available.
Mithqal Al-Fayez St, near French Embassy and Ministry of Tourism, between 3rd and 4th Circles, Jebel Amman. Tel: 06 464 2720. Fax: 06 464 7540.

Mirage £££

Very close to Abdali bus station, high-quality yet affordable with good standard rooms, parking area, rooftop barbecue, Jacuzzi and sauna.
Corner of King Hussein St and Mukhabarrat St, Jebel Weibdeh. Tel: 06 568 2000. Fax: 06 568 8890.

San Rock International £££

One of the best mid-range hotels in the capital but set a way out of town. A hundred good, spacious and spotless rooms, satellite TV and efficient service. Two restaurants, disco, coffee shop, souvenir shop, hairdresser and beauty salon.
Saeed Abu Jaber St, behind the Crowne Plaza Hotel off the 6th Circle, Jebel Amman. Tel: 06 551 3800. Email: sales@ sanrock-hotel.com

Shepherd £££

Clean and good value, this quiet 30-room hotel offers good breakfasts and consistently high standards, making it a popular choice for those in the know. Make sure you book ahead. Good restaurant, bar, café and terrace.
Zaid Bin Al-Harith St, between 1st and 2nd Circles, Jebel Amman. Tel: 06 463 9197. Fax: 06 464 2401. www.shepherd-hotel.com

Al-Qasr Howard Johnson Plaza ££££

Upper mid-range hotel with cosy, bright rooms refurbished by the Howard Johnson chain, a different style to the usual upper-end blandness. The higher rooms have balconies and fine city views. Spectacular penthouse bar and excellent restaurants. Free use of the Power Hut gym ten minutes' walk away.
3 Arroub St, Shmeisani. Tel: 06 568 9671. Fax: 06 562 0526.

Carlton ££££

Needs booking ahead since it's popular with tour groups. Offers 60 bright, airy rooms and satellite TV. Chinese restaurant, café and basement pub.
Opposite the InterContinental between the 2nd and 3rd Circles, Jebel Amman. Tel: 06 465 4200. Email: jcarlton@ joinnet.com.jo

Crowne Plaza (Amra) ££££

A cut below top-level luxury, but this hotel with 279 rooms comes with excellent facilities including a Turkish bath, Arab/Moroccan terrace, fitness centre, indoor and outdoor pools and tennis court.
King Faisal Bin Abdul Azia St, 6th Circle, Jebel Amman. Tel: 06 551 0001. www.crowneplaza.com

Four Seasons ££££

Probably the fanciest establishment in the capital, a 15-storey Art Deco palace with 193 spacious rooms equipped with all the latest luxury and gadgetry. Spa with indoor and outdoor pools, saunas and whirlpools. Free DVD rental. Wheelchair-access rooms. Opulent lobby, excellent Italian and Thai restaurants and superb bars.

Al-Kindi St, 5th Circle, Jebel Amman. Tel: 06 550 5555. Fax: 06 550 5556. www.fourseasons.com

Jordan InterContinental Hotel ££££

Well located between the 2nd and 3rd Circles, this was the first of Amman's luxury hotels and used to be called Funduq Al-Urdun (Jordan Hotel).

It is the hotel of preference for visiting top-level journalists, businesspeople and diplomats. This is why it was targeted for the bombing in summer 2005 and why there is now strict security with bag checks at the entrance. It has its own shopping arcade, one of Jordan's best bookshops, attractive lobby cafés and excellent Indian, Lebanese and Mexican restaurants. A 24-hour gym, indoor and outdoor pool, and Wi-Fi Internet too.

Al-Kulliyah Al-Islamiyah St, Jebel Amman. Tel: 06 464 1361.

Fax: 06 464 5217. www.ichotelsgroup.com/ intercontinental

Kempinski Amman ££££

Opened late 2005 in the café and restaurant quarter of Shmeisani, the Amman business district. Boasts Cuban and Italian restaurants, bowling alley, Wi-Fi, superb luxury facilities and heavily discounted rooms. Stylish Mediterranean feel with 296 bright, informal rooms and public areas. It runs six buses a day to its sister hotel on the Dead Sea, and offers two pools, a 24-hour gym and an excellent selection of Mediterranean restaurants. Possibly the best of Amman's luxury hotels for character and style.

Abdul Hamid St, Shmeisani. Tel: 06 520 0200. www. kempinski-amman.com

EATING OUT

As a rule the cheaper eateries are concentrated in downtown Amman, and are not licensed, while the upmarket places are always licensed and are situated in the

big hotels and in the business districts like Shmeisani and Abdoun.

Reem Cafeteria £

Widely considered the best *shawarma* joint in town, perfect for a late-night kebab.

2nd Circle, Jebel Amman. Tel: 06 464 5725.

Open: noon–midnight.

Lebnani Snack ££

Excellent-value Arab fast food such as falafel and cheese and olive sandwiches. Good juices are available, and the menu's in English.

Four branches around town, at Abdoun Circle, Shmeisani and downtown. Tel: 06 593 0018.

Open: noon–midnight.

L'Entrecote £££

Unassuming, quiet place offering very good French steak with perfect French fries.

At Shepherd Hotel, between the 1st and 2nd Circle. Tel: 06 464 2401.

Open: 1–3pm & 7–11pm.

Vinaigrette £££

Superb views and mellow jazz form the backdrop to this salad and sushi restaurant that also offers daily specials.

At Al-Qasr Howard Johnson Hotel, on the top floor. Tel: 06 562 0528. Open: noon–11.30pm.

Bonita Inn ££££

Spanish restaurant with excellent paella and fish, and a tapas bar beside it, with Mexican beer.
Close to the 3rd Circle, down Qas bin Sa'eda side street, Jebel Amman. Tel: 06 461 5061. Open: restaurant noon–midnight, bar 7.30pm–midnight.

Fakhr El-Din ££££

Reservations essential as this is Amman's premier restaurant, the haunt of royalty and the elite, housed in an elegant 1920s villa and offering formal Syrian cuisine. The desserts are unusually good, and in summer it is a wonderful place to dine outside among the lemon trees.
40 Taha Hussein St, behind the Iraqi Embassy, between the 1st and 2nd Circle. Tel: 06 465 2399. www.fakhreldin.com. Open: 1–3.30pm & 8pm–midnight.

Romero Restaurant ££££

Jordan's best Italian restaurant by far. Wonderful salads, seafood, pasta and risotto. Part of the Romero chain with branches in Aqaba, Pella, Umm Qais and Madaba.
Muhammad Hussein Haikal St, almost opposite the InterContinental, Jebel Amman. Tel: 06 464 4228. www.romero-jordan.com. Open: 1–3pm & 8–11pm.

Sahtain ££££

Although it can seat 400 people, this atmospheric restaurant retains a sense of intimacy through its subtly lit vaults. Excellent buffet of Arab food, with Arab music and dance.
At Kan Zaman tourist village south of Amman, near the airport. Tel: 06 412 8391. Open: 1–4pm & 7pm–midnight.

Shehrazad ££££

Evenings only, atmospheric top-floor place specialising in Moroccan cuisine with wonderful couscous and tajine dishes. Occasional live music.
At the Crowne Plaza Hotel, 6th Circle. Tel: 06 551 0001. Open: 7pm–midnight.

Tannoureen ££££

Arguably the best Arab restaurant in Jordan, offering spectacular Lebanese cuisine with an extraordinary array of *mezze* dishes. Interesting décor – with paintings of old Palestinian villages – and excellent service combine to make this a heavenly eating experience.
Shatt Al-Arab St, Souk Umm Uthayna, near the 6th Circle. Tel: 06 551 5987. Open: 1–4pm & 8–11pm.

Wild Jordan ££££

Attached to the headquarters of the Royal Society for the Conservation of Nature, this wonderful café/restaurant offers organic food with excellent salads, salmon, steaks and pasta, as well as smoothies and juices. Fabulous views of downtown Amman from the balcony. Very busy on Fridays.
Othman Bin Affan St, below the 1st Circle, Jebel Amman. Tel: 06 463 3542. www.wildjordancafe.com. Open: 11am–midnight.

ENTERTAINMENT

Cafés

Sitting in cafés watching the world go by is a major entertainment in Amman, and the following are some of the best places to do it:

Al-Rashid Court Café ££

Also called the Ecotourism Café, the entrance is down a side alley. The first-floor balcony makes an excellent viewing perch.
Al-Malek Faisal St, Downtown. Open: 10am–midnight. Closed: Fri am.

Al-Sendabad Coffee Shop ££

Good city views can be had from the roof, where you can smoke *narguileh* (water pipe) in summer.
150m (165 yards) west of the Roman theatre, Downtown. Open: 10am–midnight.

Darat Al-Funun ££

Part of the cultural centre (*see right*) this tranquil, atmospheric place beside the ruins of a Byzantine church sells coffee, tea and soft drinks. T E Lawrence is said to have written part of his *Seven Pillars of Wisdom* here.

Nimer Bin Adwan St, Downtown. Open: 10am–7pm.

Cinemas

The best ones for foreigners are:

Grand Zara (Century Cinemas)

In the Zara Centre behind the Grand Hyatt Hotel, 3rd Circle, Jebel Amman. www.century-cinemas.com

Cine Le Royal

Inside Le Royal Hotel, 3rd Circle.

Galleria

In the Sheraton Entertainment Centre, Abdoun Circle.

Grand Theatres

Boasts seven screens.
Mecca St, Mecca Mall. Tel: 06 551 8411.

Cultural centres

Darat Al-Funun (House of Arts)

Excellent complex with a small art gallery dedicated to modern Arab art, with halls for lectures, exhibitions and films.
Nimer Bin Adwan St. Tel: 06 464 3251. www.daratalfunun.org. Open: Sat–Wed 10am–

7pm, Thur 10am–8pm. Free admission.

Jordan National Gallery of Fine Arts

Displays contemporary Jordanian painting, sculpture and pottery. Attractive small gift shop and café.
Hosni Farez St, Jebel Weibdeh, signposted from King Abdullah Mosque. Tel: 06 463 0128. www.nationalgallery.org. Open: Sun–Thur 9am–5pm.

King Hussein Cultural Centre

Events are advertised in the English-language press.
Omar Matar St, Al-Muhajareen. Tel: 06 473 9953.

Royal Cultural Centre

Hosts concerts and plays.
Al-Malika Alia St, Shmeisani. Tel: 06 566 1026.

Hammam

Al-Pasha Turkish Bath

Allow two hours for the full treatment (JD15), which includes steam bath, sauna, whirlpool, 40-minute massage and two soft drinks at the end. The building faithfully recreates the

authentic Turkish bath design. There are male and female attendants and, unusually, couples are welcome during the day. Evenings tend to be men only. Book ahead to guarantee your slot.
Al-Mahmoud Taha St, Jebel Amman.
Tel: 06 463 3002. Open: 9am–2am, last booking midnight.

Nightclubs
Harir Lounge
A bit glitzy but has DJs and a live band on Mondays and Thursdays.
Abdoun Circle. Tel: 06 592 5205. Open: Mon–Fri 1pm–1am, Sat & Sun 1pm–3am.
JJ's
At its busiest on Thursday nights when Amman's beautiful people come out to play.
Grand Hyatt Hotel, Al-Hussein Bin Ali St, Jebel Amman. Open: Mon–Sat 8.30pm–2am.
Kanabaye
This place has more of a sexy, seductive feel to it, with its low orange couches (*kanabaye*), and in summer there's a pleasant outdoor terrace.

Wednesday is Ladies' Night, Thursday is Clubbing Night.
3rd Circle, Jebel Amman. Tel: 06 464 2830. Open: 8pm–1.30am.
Nai
Amazing Ottoman-style super-hip place which is a lounge, club and *mezze* bar combined. Especially busy Mondays and Thursdays, with international DJs.
Al-Qasr Howard Johnson Hotel, Shmeisani. Tel: 06 568 9671. Open: 8.30pm–2am.

Theme parks
Amman Waves
Opened summer 2007, Jordan's first water park.
15km (9 miles) south of the centre. www.ammanwaves.com
Luna Park
Offers rides and amusements for the children.
Khalid Bin Al-Walid Rd. Open: 10am–10pm. Admission charge.

SPORT AND LEISURE
Bowling
Jordan Bowling Center
Within the huge Mecca Mall, Mecca St, northwest

Amman. Tel: 06 551 2987. http://meccamall.jo
Strikers
Another good place for tenpin bowling.
In the Kempinski Hotel, Abdul Hamid Shouman Street, Shmeisani. Tel: 06 520 0200. www.kempinski-amman.com

Flying
The Royal Jordanian Gliding Club
Flights over the city.
At Marka Airport, east of Amman. Tel: 06 489 1401. www.rjglidingclub.com

Golf
Bisharat Golf Course
Jordan's only course, nine holes.
14km (9 miles) south of the city centre, signposted off the airport road. Tel: 079 552 0334.

Gyms
Club Olympus
Gym, swimming pools, whirlpool and sauna. Day passes available.
Grand Hyatt Hotel, 3rd Circle, Hussein Bin Ali Street, Jabal Amman. Tel: 06 465 1234. Open: 6am–10pm.

Power Hut

Day passes available. Easily the best gym in town.
11 August St, Shmeisani. Tel: 06 568 6349. Open: 5.30am–11pm, women only 9.30am–noon.

Horse racing
The Royal Racing Club

There is horse (and camel) racing in spring and summer, plus horse riding classes.
South of the city centre on the Desert Highway, on the way to the airport. Tel: 06 585 0630.

THE JORDAN VALLEY
Jerash
ACCOMMODATION
Olive Branch Resort £££

Secluded place in the hills with modern, clean rooms, swimming pool, games room and a good restaurant. Camping is permitted in the spacious grounds, complete with barbecue areas.
8km (5 miles) northwest of Jerash, off the road to Ajlun. Tel: 02 634 0555. Fax: 02 634 0557. www.olivebranch.com.jo

EATING OUT
Resthouse ££

With a pleasant terrace for outdoor eating, this place offers the standard range of Arab food and a full selection of *mezze.*
Within the Jerash site. Open: 8am–8pm.

Ajlun
ACCOMMODATION
Qal'at Al-Jabal ££

Simple, clean rooms with fine views. Needs booking ahead in the summer months. There's a lovely terrace where meals are served in summer.
On the quiet road 1km (2/3 mile) before Ajlun Castle. Tel: 02 642 0202. www.jabal-hotel.com

Pella
ACCOMMODATION
Pella Countryside Hotel ££

Run by the Pella Resthouse manager (*see right*), offering seven simple, traditional rooms with private bathroom and hot shower. Good breakfast and family ambience.

On the hillside above the site. Tel: 02 217 555. www.romero-jordan.com

EATING OUT
Pella Resthouse £££

Stunning place with one of Jordan's most atmospheric terraces gazing down over the site. Cold beers, fresh juices and Jordan's freshest fish caught daily from the river. Chilled Cremisan white wine from Bethlehem complements it perfectly.
On the hillside above the site. Tel: 02 217 555. www.romero-jordan.com. Open: 8am–sunset.

Umm Qais
EATING OUT
Resthouse £££

Restored Ottoman building with a terrace offering views over Lake Tiberias and the Golan Heights. Superb food from the Italian Romero chain.
Within the Umm Qais site. Tel: 02 750 0555. www.romero-jordan.com. Open: 10am–sunset, except Thursdays and Fridays when you can book ahead for an evening meal.

Irbid
ACCOMMODATION
Al-Joud Hotel £££
This is Irbid's best hotel, used by visiting academics. Clean, spacious rooms with satellite TV, friendly service, a downstairs café and an extensive room-service menu.
Off University St, opposite the university mosque. Tel: 02 727 5515.

THE DESERT PALACES
Qasr Azraq
ACCOMMODATION
Azraq Eco-lodge ££
A colonial-style 1940s former British military hospital, restored and renovated into an eco-lodge by a Jordanian architect. There are 16 air-conditioned military-themed rooms with private bathrooms. Kitchen and restaurant offering Chechen cuisine cooked by a local Chechen family. Eco-friendly design. The place is run by the Royal Society for the Conservation of Nature, in conjunction with the tour group Wild Jordan.

Signposted south off a side road 600m (1/3 mile) after the T-junction arrival at Azraq. Tel: 06 461 6523. www.rscn.org.jo. Email: tourism@rscn.org.jo

EATING OUT
Azraq Eco-lodge £££
The best place by far, and, if you are not staying, they will still feed you if you telephone in advance (*see details above*).
Open: noon–3pm & 7–9pm.

Qasr Al-Kharraneh
EATING OUT
Simple refreshments are available beside the Visitor Centre in a black Bedouin goat-hair tent.
Open: 8.30am–6pm (summer), 8.30am–4pm (winter).

THE KING'S HIGHWAY
Madaba
EATING OUT
Haret Jdoudna £££
A sophisticated complex of craft shops, bars, cafés, pizzerias and restaurants set in an old restored house. Traditional Arab cuisine indoors and in the courtyard, with a small wine bar.
Talal St. Tel: 05 324 8650. Open: 11am–midnight.

The Dead Sea
ACCOMMODATION
Dead Sea Mövenpick ££££
Supremely elegant top-class hotel complete with Damascene wooden ceiling in the bar. Rooms in two-storey buildings arranged in a succession of village-like courtyards. The exclusive Zara Spa is off to one side. Complex of nine bars and restaurants.
Swaimeh, Dead Sea Road. Tel: 05 356 1111. www.moevenpick-deadsea.com

Jordan Valley Marriott Resort and Spa ££££
Spectacular hotel built in a U-shape round three pools (including an infinity pool) overlooking the Dead Sea. Twelve cafés and restaurants, two cinemas, tennis court and an amphitheatre arena. On-site spa with full range of treatments.
Swaimeh, Dead Sea Road. Tel: 05 356 0400. www.marriott.com

Kempinski Hotel Ishtar ££££

Between the Mövenpick and the Dead Sea Spa Hotel, this is the latest addition to the top-range luxury spa hotels found in this area.
Swaimeh, Dead Sea Road. Tel: 05 356 8888. www.kempinski.com. Email: sales.ishtar@ kempinski.com

EATING OUT

Apart from the excellent restaurants of the luxury hotels on the shoreline, there is also the **Dead Sea Panorama** (*open: 11am–9pm*), set about 5km (3 miles) above the Dead Sea on the new road up to Madaba. Part of a complex with a Dead Sea Museum, the restaurant offers superb international cuisine and diners enjoy spectacular views.

Zerqa Ma'in

ACCOMMODATION

Evason Ma'In Hot Springs ££££
Located by itself in a highly exclusive dead-end road that forks off left as you descend from Madaba to the Dead Sea, this superb complex functions year-round, offering three hot springs and comfortable en-suite rooms.
Tel: 05 324 5500. www.sixsenses.com. Email: reservations-main@sixsenses.com

Kerak

ACCOMMODATION

Kerak Resthouse £££
Has 17 rooms fully refurbished in 2005 to a high standard, with the Kan Zaman restaurant opposite on its own terrace overlooking the castle.
Right beside the castle, PO Box 107, Kerak. Tel: 03 235 1148. Email: kerakcastle@gmail.com

EATING OUT

Kan Zaman £££
With its own fine terrace, this place offers very good Arab buffets when there are tour groups, or à la carte for individuals. It is run by the Kerak Resthouse (*see above*), just a few metres away.
Open: 11.30am–8.30pm.

PETRA

ACCOMMODATION

There are around 70 hotels in the Petra area now, and in low season (June–Aug & Nov–Feb) hefty discounts can be negotiated. The following is a selection of recommended ones:

Ammareen Camp £
This rather wonderful place is the only campsite in the Petra area. It's a Bedouin-style permanent encampment of goat-hair tents, run by the local Ammareen tribe. Located in its own little valley near Siq Al-Barid (Little Petra), you will need your own transport or taxi to reach it, but it makes a total getaway from the crowds of Wadi Musa. There are proper flushing loos and running hot and cold water. Meals can be arranged with prior notice.
Tel: 079 975 5551. Fax: 06 593 6359. www.bedouincamp.net

Musa Springs ££
Right up at the start of the village of Wadi Musa, next to the spring of Moses, this backpackers' favourite

gives free transport down to the site entrance and back. Breakfast costs extra but packed lunches can be arranged with prior notice. Rooms with en-suite or shared facilities. Laundry facilities and budget rooftop sleeping in high summer.
Tel: 03 215 6310. Email: musaspring_hotel@yahoo. co.uk

Petra Moon Hotel £££
Located up behind the Mövenpick, quite close to the site entrance, this place offers simple, clean rooms with clean en-suites.
Tel/Fax: 03 215 6220. Email: petramoonhotel@ yahoo.com

Petra Palace Hotel £££
Located 500m (1/3 mile) from the site entrance, this is good value with some rooms opening out on to a terrace with a pool. Pleasant restaurant and bar.
Tel: 03 215 6723. www.petrapalace.com.jo

Crowne Plaza Resort Hotel ££££
The old Petra forum, this was the first luxury-end hotel in Petra. Along

with its sister premises, the old Petra Resthouse, it is located virtually in the site itself, directly above the Nabatean Cave Bar. The actual hotel is quite bland with unexceptional food and service, but the terrace overlooking the weird rocks of Petra, with its small, outdoor, year-round heated pool, is one of the most atmospheric places in the country to sit and sip refreshments.
Tel: 03 215 6266. Fax: 03 215 6977. www.crowneplaza.com

Mövenpick ££££
One of the most spectacular hotels in the Middle East, designed in traditional Damascene style with four-storey atrium and mosaic-tiled fountain. Excellent location just a few metres from the Petra ticket office and entrance.
Tel: 03 215 7111. Fax: 03 215 7112. www. moevenpick-petra.com

Sofitel Taybet Zaman ££££
Wonderfully stylish hotel tucked away in an unlikely location in

Tayibah village, 11km (7 miles) from Petra. The old Ottoman houses of the village have been renovated and redesigned to afford single-storey, cottage-like rooms, extremely spacious with traditional furnishings and beautifully presented. The hotel has a Turkish bath with a trained masseur, an excellent, atmospheric restaurant with some of the best food in Jordan, and a series of shops selling local handicrafts and Dead Sea products. There are 105 rooms and a royal suite, satellite TV, and an outdoor pool which functions April–October. The hotel sits at a high altitude so it's much cooler than in Petra and Wadi Musa.
Tel: 03 215 0111. Email: reservation@ taybetzaman.com

EATING OUT
Mystic Pizza ££
Simple unlicensed place near the site entrance serving pizzas and pasta dishes.
Open: 10am–11pm.

Petra Palace Hotel ££££
Boasting Wadi Musa's
liveliest bar, with the
local strong brew, Petra,
8 per cent alcohol.
Tel: 03 215 6723.
www.petrapalace.com.jo.
Email: ppwnwm@go.
com.jo. Open: noon–11pm.
Al-Saraya ££££
Fabulously varied buffet
for a mega-blowout meal
to reward yourself after
the exertions of the day's
sightseeing.
In the Mövenpick.
Tel: 03 215 7111.
Open: noon–11pm.
Sandstone
Restaurant ££££
Pleasant outdoor seating
with excellent meals and
buffets, next door to the
Oriental Restaurant, not
far from the site entrance.
Tel: 03 215 7701.
Open: 8.30am–9pm.

ENTERTAINMENT
Petra offers very little in
the nightlife department
beyond what is available
in the various hotels, but
it may be the perfect
place to experience a full
Turkish bath. The best
places are **Petra Turkish
Bath** (*Tel: 03 215 7085.*
Open: 10am–11pm) in

the passage under the
Silk Road Hotel, and the
ones in the **Amra Palace
Hotel** (*Tel: 03 215 7070.*
www.amrapalace.com)
with separate men's and
women's sections. The
Sofitel Taybet Zaman
(*see p169*) also has an
excellent Turkish bath,
but only available for
use by guests. The
professional male
masseur works on
women as well as men
without turning a hair.

WADI RUM
ACCOMMODATION
Bait Ali Desert Camp ££
This extraordinary place
offers an interesting
alternative to staying in
the permanent camps
that tour groups use
within Wadi Rum itself.
It is signposted off the
Rum access road, some
6km (4 miles) from the
Rum Visitor Centre.
As well as tented
accommodation and
chalets, it offers Rum's
first swimming pool. The
Swalhiyeen tribe who run
the place offer unique
camel rides or 4WD trips
in the nearby desert
landscapes at cheaper

rates than those offered
by the Visitor Centre.
Tel: 03 202 2626.
www.baitali.com

EATING OUT
The **Visitor Centre** at
Wadi Rum has a fine and
surprisingly stylish
restaurant with an
attractive outdoor seating
area. Arab cuisine.
www.wadirum.jo.
Open: 9am–6pm.

AQABA
ACCOMMODATION
Aqaba Star ££
Adequate rooms with
balconies overlooking
the sea and the street.
The best of Aqaba's
bottom-end
accommodation.
Corniche, town centre.
Tel: 03 201 6480.
Coral Bay Hotel ££££
This hotel has 69 clean
and pleasant rooms on a
quiet beach well away
from the bustle of Aqaba.
At the Royal Diving Club,
17km (10½ miles) south
of town. Tel: 03 201 7035.
Fax: 03 201 7097.
**Aquamarina 1 Beach
Club Hotel ££££**
Best value in its range,
with its own beach,

diving centre and watersports. Lots of bars make it popular with visiting US Navy crews on shore leave.

Corniche, North Coast, between the Radisson and the InterContinental. Tel: 03 210 6250. Fax: 03 203 2630.

InterContinental ££££
Ultra-plush hotel in prime location. The InterContinental offers beautifully landscaped gardens overlooking the sea. Lavish rooms with Wi-Fi, private beach, six restaurants and its own marina.
Tel: 03 209 2222. www. intercontinental.com. Email: info@icaqaba.com

Kempinski Aqaba ££££
Opened mid-2009, this new luxury hotel offers rooms and suites with Red Sea views. It also boasts an extensive range of leisure facilities.
King Hussein St. Tel: 03 209 0888. www. kempinski-aqaba.com

Mövenpick Resort Hotel ££££
Vast and lavish hotel in Moroccan style offering three restaurants and

four cafés. Guests can enjoy the huge pool and beach complex across the bridge with three pools, a gym and magnificent gardens.
King Hussein St. Tel/Fax: 03 203 4020. www.moevenpick-aqaba.com

EATING OUT
Aqaba's seafood is very good but can be expensive, especially the lobster.

Ös Urfa Restaurant ££
A Turkish place with a range of *mezze*, good grills and main courses of 1,001-things-to-do-with-an-aubergine.
King Hussein St. Tel: 03 614 6020. Open: 9am–midnight.

Syrian Palace Restaurant ££
Next to Al-Amer Hotel, this unlicensed place does good-value Syrian and Jordanian food, including fish.
Raghadan St. Tel: 03 201 4788. Open: 11am–11pm.

Ali Baba Restaurant £££
Long-established place in the town centre with pleasant outdoor seating.

Grilled meat and fish, *mezze*, as well as cakes and breakfast food.
Raghadan St. Tel: 03 201 3901. Open: 8am–midnight.

Flocka Restaurant ££££
Upmarket seafood restaurant with indoor and outdoor seating. Accepts credit cards.
An-Nahda St. Tel: 03 203 0860. Open: 12.30pm–11.30pm.

Royal Yacht Club ££££
With a terrace overlooking the marina, this is part of the excellent Italian Romero chain, offering superb pizzas, pasta, *mezze* and fish. Probably Aqaba's best restaurant.
Off the main Corniche roundabout in the town centre. Tel: 03 202 2404. www.romero-jordan.com. Open: 11.30am–3.30pm & 7.30–11.30pm.

Silk Road Restaurant ££££
One of Aqaba's finest places with wonderful seafood salads, chowders and main courses. Three dining areas and nightly Russian belly dancers in summer.

As-Sa'dah St.
Tel: 03 203 3556.
Open: noon–midnight.

ENTERTAINMENT
Aqaba Gateway
A shopping complex with a good collection of restaurants, fast-food outlets, shops, bars and a cinema.
Al-Baladiah Circle.
Tel: 03 201 2200.

Cafés and ice-cream parlours
The beachfront cafés along the Aqaba promenade are wonderful places to sit and while away the time, so close to the water you can almost dip your toes in.

Aqaba Turkish Baths
Women need to arrange it in advance, but this place offers the full massage, scrubbing and steam bath, a wonderfully rejuvenating experience and highly recommended.
King Hussein St.
Tel: 03 203 1605. Open: 9am–9pm.

Jordan Experience
This is a multimedia experience showing three times a day, simulating a flying-carpet tour of Jordan, with elements of Disney.
Inside Aqaba Gateway, Al-Baladiah Circle.
Tel: 03 202 2200. Email: jex@aqabagateway.com. Admission charge.

Nightlife
The luxury hotels all have bars and many have a happy hour from 6 to 7.30pm.

Aquamarina 1 Beach Club Hotel
It's generally reckoned to have the most lively nightclub, with cabaret acts and even belly dancing (*see listing pp170–71*).

Baranda Lounge
Inside Aqaba Gateway (*see listing pp171–2*), this is a relaxed bar with an attractive terrace and patio to catch the breezes. Food is served till midnight and you can get bar snacks till 3am.

Fun Pub
Probably the most fun of the hotel bars, with a happy hour from 8 to 9pm.
In the Mövenpick (see listing p171).
Tel: 03 203 4020.
Open: 8pm–2am.

Royal Yacht Club
This is above the Romero Restaurant in the marina, and is the most up-market night-time venue for a more sophisticated drink (*see listing p171*).
Tel: 03 202 2404.

SPORT AND LEISURE
Cruises
Sindbad
Sunset cruises on Thursday and Friday afternoons, and a snorkelling trip with lunch included. These trips can usually be booked from your hotel. The glass-bottom boats are quite fun for those who do not want to enter the water, but the amount of coral and sea life that can be seen this way is disappointingly little.
Booth inside the Aqaba Gateway complex (see listing pp171–2).
Tel: 03 205 0077.
www.sindbadjo.com

Diving
Aqaba International Dive Center
This small centre runs the full PADI course, is well equipped and arranges all transportation.

Friendly staff and experienced guides.
Off King Hussein St, beside Aqaba Gulf Hotel. Tel: 03 203 1213. www. aqabadivingcenter.com

Arab Divers

This friendly dive centre offers multilingual instructors and PADI courses. Beach dives only.
King Hussein St. Tel: 03 203 1808. Email: arabdivers@hotmail.com

Dive Aqaba

Boat dives and courses at all levels. Run by a joint British-Jordanian team, this is possibly the best outfit in the country and is highly recommended.
Opposite the Golden Tulip Hotel. Tel: 03 203 4849. www.diveaqaba.com

Red Sea Diving Centre

This is one of the most long-standing dive centres in town.
Off King Hussein St. Tel: 03 202 2323.

Royal Diving Club

This is the only dive centre actually located out on the reefs. As well as the full dives, you can simply hire a mask, flippers and snorkel for the day from their jetty. Admission to the Royal

Diving Club beach costs JD5 and includes sunbed, towel and return transport to town.
17km (10½ miles) south of Aqaba, beside the Coral Bay Hotel. Tel: 03 201 7035. www.rdc.jo. Email: info@rdc.jo

Seastar

A long-established dive centre in one of Aqaba's best-known hotels, it uses the hotel's private beach at Club Murjan on the south-coast reefs. Offers snorkelling, diving and various courses. A shuttle bus runs between the hotel and Club Murjan several times a day, and, if you are a hotel guest, prices for both the room and the diving are discounted.
At the Alcazar Hotel, town centre. Tel: 03 201 4131. www.aqabadiving seastar.com

Watersports

The bigger hotels offer waterskiing, jet-skiing, windsurfing and kayaking, with **Club Murjan** (of the Alcazar Hotel), the **Aquamarina 1 Beach Club Hotel** and **Barracuda Beach** having the biggest range.

DANA

ACCOMMODATION

Faynan Wilderness Lodge ££

Set down in the Dana Reserve, this lodge offers 26 rooms, no electricity, and is lit by candlelight at night. Peaceful, calm ambience, with meals prepared in the communal eating area. A memorable experience.
RSCN; same details as Dana Guesthouse below.

RSCN Dana Guesthouse ££

Nine beautifully designed rooms and terrace with stunning views overlooking the Wadi Dana. Clean and simple, and needs to be booked weeks ahead. Only one en-suite room. Good breakfast and meals by arrangement, plus a shop selling local produce.
Tel: 03 227 0497. www.rscn.org.jo. Email: tourism@rscn.org.jo

EATING OUT

The only food available is in the hotels and lodges within the reserve, arranged by advance booking.

Index

176

10/11

Acknowledgements

Thomas Cook Publishing wishes to thank DIANA DARKE, to whom the copyright belongs, for the photographs in this book, except for the following images:

DREAMSTIME Photomaru 1, Jasmina 54, Macsim 130
ISTOCKPHOTO.COM Hanoded Photography 47
PICTURES COLOUR LIBRARY Simon Heaton 131
WIKIMEDIA COMMONS Helene C. Stikkel (DoD) 30, World Economic Forum 31, Thomas Bantle 78, Mohammed Al Momany (NOAA) 119

For CAMBRIDGE PUBLISHING MANAGEMENT LIMITED:
Project editor: Kate Taylor
Typesetter: Paul Queripel
Proofreaders: Ed Robinson & Cath Senker
Indexer: Karolin Thomas

SEND YOUR THOUGHTS TO
BOOKS@THOMASCOOK.COM

We're committed to providing the very best up-to-date information in our travel guides and constantly strive to make them as useful as they can be. You can help us to improve future editions by letting us have your feedback. If you've made a wonderful discovery on your travels that we don't already feature, if you'd like to inform us about recent changes to anything that we do include, or if you simply want to let us know your thoughts about this guidebook and how we can make it even better – we'd love to hear from you.

Send us ideas, discoveries and recommendations today and then look out for your valuable input in the next edition of this title.

Emails to the above address, or letters to the traveller guides Series Editor, Thomas Cook Publishing, PO Box 227, Coningsby Road, Peterborough PE3 8SB, UK.

Please don't forget to let us know which title your feedback refers to!